"Bird's Eye View of El Paso, Texas in 1885" as drawn by August Koch.

THE STATE NATIONAL—SINCE 1881

STATE NATIONAL BANK
STATE NATIONAL BANK
RIO GRANDE
PHARMACY
HARNESS BOOT SHOP

The State National
SINCE 1881
The Pioneer Bank of El Paso

BY

C. L. SONNICHSEN

AND

M. G. McKINNEY

El Paso : TEXAS WESTERN PRESS : 1971

Designed by
CARL HERTZOG

Library of Congress Catalog Card No. 78-139681
SBN 87404-028-0

INTRODUCTION

• THE STORY OF A BANKING ENTERPRISE *could easily be dull and deadly — a chronicle of dividends and interest rates, profits on government and municipal bonds, bad loans and defaulted mortgages. In reality it need be no such thing. A bank is an important and necessary human institution. It may be true that only bankers and their stockholders really love it, but in our form of society nobody can do without it unless he revolts against all social order and goes to live in an abandoned automobile in a junkyard. And even there he might find a little money a great comfort. A civilized community without a bank would be unthinkable and anything indispensable will always be interesting.*

The right way to look at a bank is to begin with what it deals in — cash and credit. Since the community is an organism, something like the human body, the bank is the heart and money is the blood. As long as the blood flows, the body is alive. When it stops flowing, the situation is desperate. Hence a bank's first concern is to stay solvent and operative. The heart must go on beating, because the body depends on it. This explains why bankers are usually conservative and careful and unwilling to take unnecessary risks. An adventurous bank may be open today and closed tomorrow.

This point can hardly be overemphasized. Folklore — meaning ideas which we accept without examination—assumes that a banker is a flint-hearted Scrooge who thinks only of his own profits and ignores the needs of everybody else. Eugene Manlove Rhodes, whose novels about the cattlemen of southern New Mexico have been highly praised, thinks all money lenders are grasping and crooked. Of one of them he says, "He reminds me of a rainy day in a goat shed." Of a banker at Alamogordo (who robs his own bank) he remarks, "His mind is too ballbearing altogether."

Mr. Rhodes needed to sit down and talk to a live, reasonable, conscientious banker and see the thing from his point of view. He would have learned that bankers are not as black as they are painted. Their hearts are no harder than other men's; they like to be helpful and obliging on occasion. But they can't bet on lost causes since the first duty of a bank is to stay alive.

Its second duty is to build confidence and trust. Every one of its functions — borrowing and lending, foreign exchange, real-estate mortgages, safekeeping, Trust Department business — all are based on confidence. What happens when confidence fails is a sad part of the history of the twenties and thirties in El Paso and elsewhere, a part which gives extra significance to the fact that The State National Bank of El Paso is the sole survivor of something like a dozen banks which opened here in the early days, the only one in which confidence did not fail.

The third duty of a bank is to understand community needs and push constructive enterprises, giving support where it is needed and deserved. Healthy banks can function best in healthy communities, and it is part of the bank's function to promote community health.

For the stockholders, of course, the primary purpose of a bank is to pay dividends, and bankers like to make little speeches to this effect at stockholders' meetings. But in their hearts, if they are good bankers, they know that even in a bank money is not everything — not nearly everything. Service and character and responsibility and honesty and dedication, all the old virtues which we hardly dare to mention any more, are the real business of any public institution, be it library, church, supermarket, city council, or bank — but especially a bank.

This helps to account for the peculiar feeling one has when he steps inside a fine bronze-and-marble bank building. People come close to being reverent there, or at least a little solemn. Everybody catches the feeling, all those busy souls scurrying about, intent on their business: gnarled old men and bird-like little old ladies; merchants and professors and housewives; little people and important people; even the bank officers hurrying from one department to another with zeal in their eyes and priceless papers in their hands. The employees wear suits and are careful of haircuts and shoeshines. Nobody makes loud noises or stops to engage in casual conversation. The atmosphere is not quite as reverent as in the Episcopal Church around the corner, but it comes close.

And why not? Money is serious business. It involves life savings and grocery bills and trips back home to see Mother and Dad; a college education for Junior; the possibility of doing or being something better than we did or were yesterday. Economists may tell us, "It's only money." But people who don't have much of it don't talk or think that way. When Raymond Adams took over the Savings Department of The State National Bank in 1948, Vice-President Guyler Magruder said to him, "You take good care of those accounts. Nothing means more to people than their savings. Savings come first; their wives come second."

"When you watch those people come in on a hot summer day with a dollar or two, stand in line to put it in their savings account, and then go home in the simmering heat," says Adams, "you know that Guyler was at least half right."

Bankers are well aware that their business is a matter of life and death to hundreds of people and they feel an obligation to make their surroundings as dignified as possible. They don't ordinarily go in for stained-glass windows, but they might as well. Any borrower or would-be-borrower recognizes the similarity between a loan officer's desk and the confessional. A vice-president in charge of personal loans can bare your soul just about as quickly as a priest can.

This is a bank as seen by people on the outside. Viewed from the inside, it is a much livelier and more human place. Like a transatlantic liner or a hospital or a department store, it is a little world spinning on its own axis, involved in its own private life, full of human loyalties and frustrations, ambitions and aspirations, triumphs and failures — love, hate, grief, joy, death. There is a hierarchy, slowly but constantly shifting and changing, a ladder which everybody is trying to climb with the Chairman of the Board at the top and runners and mail boys and check rackers at the bottom. It can and does generate the most intense loyalty in long-time employees who, as one of them puts it, "seem to think Heaven is going to look like The State National Bank." And you meet a few who can't stand the place and have to get out.

When the bank is an old one with memories that go back a long time — scandals and odd happenings and anecdotes that the patri-

archs like to chuckle over — somebody ought to gather it all together and make it part of the larger pattern of history.

It has been ninety years since The State National Bank of El Paso was founded — real antiquity in a country as new as the American Southwest. It has survived some strenuous times since it was organized before the railroad came. It has grown with its city, served its city, and shared in every worthwhile enterprise that the city has undertaken. It is a little democracy in the midst of increasing paternalism and socialism. It cares for the moral and professional development of its employees as few organizations continue to do in our time — cherishes them and rewards them as they duly deserve. Any venerable association of men is well worth a history. The State National Bank of El Paso, our oldest business firm, has a special right to have its story told.

CONTENTS

PHOTOGRAPHS

THE STATE NATIONAL—SINCE 1881

CHAPTER I

THE BIRTH OF A BANK

FEBRUARY OF 1880 was a frigid, uncomfortable month all over Texas.[1] When the Overland stage (a spring wagon with a canvas top) pulled into El Paso at 7:30 on the evening of February 12, the three passengers were weary and chilled but glad to be alive. There had been an Indian scare a hundred miles back at Fort Quitman. Mrs. Rohman's one-story adobe hotel, where the Mills Building stands now, was a real haven for men nine days out from Fort Worth. They climbed stiffly down and went inside as the stage moved on to its 'dobe-walled corral a long block away on San Francisco Street. One of the travelers, a Mr. Ponder, disappears into the West Texas twilight at this point. The other two, without realizing it, had come home. We still read their names on streets and schools and office buildings. The signatures they placed on Mrs. Rohman's register read: *Charles R. Morehead, Leavenworth, Kansas; Oscar T. Bassett, Fort Worth, Texas.*[2]

Mr. Morehead, a small, wiry, intense man with a Kentucky-Colonel goatee, was an extraordinary person who at forty-two had lived one full life already and was about to embark on another. Bassett was a stocky fellow with a heavy mustache, a shrewd eye, and a quiet manner. At thirty he was a successful businessman, a contractor and lumber dealer who had left Indiana only a short time before and established a lumber yard in Fort Worth. There he and Morehead had made contact, exactly how we do not know, and he had come along to look for business opportunities in the new country.

Morehead, a careful and far-seeing man, had planned this trip with his usual meticulousness. He had passes on stage and railroad and letters of introduction to important people, but neither he nor Bassett had thought of El Paso as much more than an overnight stop. Who would have expected to find anything of interest in this straggling adobe village, more Mexican than American, lost in the Great American Desert hundreds of miles from any important center of population? They were there in the first place because officials of the Texas and Pacific Railroad had commissioned Morehead to gather information about new construction they were planning. Would it be practical, they wished to know, to start road-building crews eastward from El Paso while other crews built westward from Fort Worth? At the same time Morehead was carrying out a mission for a group of St. Louis capitalists, related to him through business or family ties, who wanted a report on the feasibility of investment in the booming Arizona silver mines.

They had survived a rough trip. When they climbed into the Concord coach at the Fort Worth station on Tuesday, February 3, an unprecedented snowfall had left twelve frigid inches on the ground. Two days out, they changed to a "celerity wagon," a light vehicle with a canvas top which was easier on the mules or broncos but harder on the passengers. As they rocked and jolted deeper into the treeless, uninhabited wilds, their peace of mind was eroded by one of their fellow passengers, a Mr. Corbett, who told tales of Indian attacks and escapes – adventures which Mr. Morehead found, as he commented ironically in his diary, "very comforting."

Only a month before, two mining engineers en route from Colorado to San Antonio had run into a band of Chief Victorio's Apaches at Crow Spring on the west side of the Guadalupe Mountains. They managed to save their lives but lost their horses and had to walk the hundred miles back to the Ranger camp at Ysleta.[3] Where were those Indians now? They loved to ambush travelers between Fort Davis and the first settlements in the Rio Grande Valley, the very route the stage was following.

Soon after the travelers left Fort Davis, they ran into a sandstorm with a bitter wind behind it. Sometimes the mules would not go on in the face of that bitter blast. It was worse when they reached old Fort Quitman, in 1880 a stage station beside the Rio Grande where the El Paso road turned northwest and began to follow the river. While the mules were being changed, the men gulped down a "meal" of bread and black coffee – all the station keeper could offer – and learned that Apaches might be lying in wait ahead. The day before, the Indians had driven off a herd of sheep. The three passengers kept their guns handy after the driver called "All Aboard" and agreed that in case of attack they would jump out into the thick tornillo brush, keep together, and make the best fight they could. Morehead tells what happened next:

> About six or eight miles out the driver handed us the reins and said, "Camp fire smouldering." He lit a match the usual cowboy way and looked around the camp, and came bounding in the wagon and said, "Moccasin tracks, Gentlemen," and lit out all the mules could stand. We had one change of horses between there and El Paso, where we arrived at 7:30 p.m.

Morehead was not nearly as nervous as the driver. He had been at home in Indian country since he was nineteen years old and had had his share of narrow escapes and close calls. Born in Missouri in 1836, he absorbed the practical part of his education in his father's banking and mercantile business in Lexington. The academic part he picked up in the public school and at an academy known as the Masonic College in the same town. In 1852, just sixteen years old, he went to work as a clerk in a Lexington store and three years later he found a place with Russell, Majors and Waddell.

This famous firm was in the business of freighting supplies to the army posts in the wilderness west of the Missouri settlements, and the employees had to be men of considerable courage and character. Apparently young Morehead had what it took. November of 1856 saw him on the road as assistant wagon master in charge of thirty-five wagons loaded with corn for Fort Kearny, Wyoming. A band of roving Indians stopped the train and scared everybody, but they accepted presents of flour, sugar and coffee and went away peaceably. On the return trip the Pawnees proved less tractable, robbing the wagons of provisions and slaughtering the animals for sport.

The following winter Morehead made the long haul to Fort Bridger, Wyoming. En route, he lost the beef cattle he was driving to a band of hungry red men, but the small escort went in pursuit and got the livestock back. Before the party could catch its breath, a company of 150 Mormon scouts from Salt Lake City surrounded the camp, burned some of the wagons, took most of the stock they had just reclaimed from the Indians, and demanded all the arms the group carried. The convoy was saved by a group of soldiers and went on to complete its business, but on the journey home Morehead stood off more Indians and a pack of hungry wolves.

His descendants say that his next venture took him all the way to Salt Lake City, where he met and became friendly with Brigham Young. The return trip was made in the dead of winter – a journey which many said was impossible. By this time, Russell, Majors, and Waddell were talking about starting the Pony Express and they sent Morehead to Washington, as one who had been over the route in all weathers, to report to President Buchanan and the Postal authorities.[4]

This was in 1858. In 1861, in carrying out a contract to deliver cattle to Forts Larned and Lyon, in Kansas, he almost lost his life to Indians again. Two years later he penetrated even farther into wild country, making a trip to New Mexico for reasons which his biographers do not make clear.[5] In 1868-69 he served as Mayor of Leavenworth, Kansas.

In all he spent over twenty-five years in close contact with the Great Plains and their inhabitants, both red and white. "He played a rough game among rough men," said his friend, Editor J. D. Ponder of the El Paso *Times*, many years later. "His moral and physical courage was proved again and again. . . . He carried his life in his pistol holster; but in the drawing room of culture, he was a model of courtly dignity."[6]

He was actually a very proud and sensitive man, not easy to know but a devoted and loyal friend once you got to know him. His frontier experiences made him skeptical of the goodness of human nature. They likewise made him unwilling to interfere in other people's personal business, good or bad. He was always suspicious of reformers and dogooders. These characteristics were to have far-reaching effects on the course of events in his adopted town in the years that were ahead. There was never any question, of course, about his personal morality and integrity.

In 1859 he married Lemire Morris. Her family was related to William Morris, the financier of the American Revolution,[7] but she grew up on a plantation near Maysville, Kentucky. Orphaned and poor, she took charge of her three younger sisters after the Civil War and brought them to Lexington, Missouri. The Moreheads were distantly related to the Morrises and it was natural that Charles and Lemire should meet.[8]

The wedding not merely made him a happy man but it connected him with a number of people who were to be important in his life. Two of the Morris sisters married the Newman brothers, H. L. (Henry) and E. S. (Zeke) – cattle kings and frontier capitalists. Morehead undoubtedly knew them already. H. L. worked in a store in Lexington and went out on the plains for Russell, Majors and Waddell, just as Morehead had done. In 1862 he moved to Leavenworth to become a freighter on his own hook, and in 1867 opened a bank there. At one time he and his brothers owned vast cattle ranches in Wyoming and Nebraska. The hard winter of 1886-87 hurt them and changing times persuaded them to cut down their ranch holdings, but they continued to invest in land and banks and livestock. In 1874 H. L. Newman founded the bank at National Stockyards, Illinois. Both H. L. and E. S. Newman became El Paso residents eventually, thanks to Morehead's trip in 1880, and their descendants are still important contributors to the life of the town.[9]

It was the Newmans and their friends and associates in Missouri, particularly in St. Louis, who commissioned Morehead to see if money could be made in the Arizona mines. They saw no reason for letting the Guggenheims have it all, and they acquired options on property at Globe and Tombstone.

Bassett was not interested in mining but hoped to find other business opportunities in the new country. He was an orphan boy from Vermont who seems to have been born with an instinct for getting things done and for making money in the process. At the age of fourteen he enlisted in the Union army but was sent home when his officers had time to take a good look at him. Settling in Clinton, Indiana, he learned to handle tools and men and became first a contractor and then a lumber dealer. A year or so before his trip West with Morehead, he moved to Fort Worth and established a lumber business there, but he kept up his Indiana connections. His wife was Myrtle Nebeker, a vivacious and charming blonde of Dutch ancestry whose gaiety offset the taciturnity of her husband.

She was one of the first women graduates of the University of Indiana and one of the earliest members of the Kappa Alpha Theta sorority. Myrtle Avenue in El Paso was named for her. Unfortunately her health was precarious and she dreaded leaving home. Mr. Bassett was thus obliged to keep a foot in both camps.[10]

On their stagecoach trip to and beyond El Paso, Morehead and Bassett got on wonderfully together, perhaps because neither of them was particularly sociable and each was willing to let the other alone. Morehead said when the trip was over, "We never passed a cross word and remained friends until the end. But few men ever passed over so much country almost uninhabited in a primitive way without accident."[11]

From February 13 to February 19 – just a week – Morehead and Bassett stayed in El Paso and "viewed the adobe city" (Morehead's words). They visited Paso del Norte across the river and were entertained there to their great satisfaction. They had dinner with Joseph Magoffin and Judge Allen Blacker, old-time residents with unshakable faith in the future of the community. They drove out to the Pass, where the river broke through the mountain wall, and they looked at some of the land which was for sale in the Valley. They listened and they pondered. They talked to excited people on El Paso Street who were sure the railroads were going to make everybody rich. They could see that something was about to happen to this frontier hamlet – something important. "Plenty of room here for a big city," Morehead wrote in his diary, "which it will be in time after the railroads come. It is the natural pass from East to West, North and South, and it may become a mining center."

The day before the two men left, they bought 400 acres of land from Joseph Magoffin. The purchase committed them to something, though they were not quite sure yet what it would be.

At 6:30 p.m. on February 19 they took the stage for points farther west, spent over two weeks looking at mines and related enterprises at Florence, Globe, Charleston, Tombstone and other places in Arizona, and finally caught the train for Los Angeles and San Francisco. Even in California, however, El Paso was on Morehead's mind, and he kept looking for information about the place. When he called on A. N. Towne, General Manager of the Southern

Pacific Railroad, in San Francisco, the subject came up. "He gave us much encouragement about El Paso and told us of the railroads then building there," Morehead recorded, "which information and acquaintance proved of value to both of us."

By the time the travelers reached St. Louis on March 27, they had made up their minds. They were going to West Texas within the year, and for good. Bassett went on to Indiana to join his wife. Morehead reported to the St. Louis group. His diary entry for March 31 begins: "In St. Louis. Talked over matters in El Paso with Mr. Rankin, Newman, Orrick, and others and decided to open a National Bank in El Paso."

So the die was cast. On Morehead's advice the options on the Arizona mining properties were dropped and negotiations were started which, hopefully, would lead to a charter for the new bank.

The approach was deliberate, to say the least. John C. Orrick, a prominent St. Louis lawyer, got around to writing a letter in October, seven months after the decision was made. Instead of addressing the Comptroller of the Currency directly, he asked E. D. Jones of No. 1 Wall Street to handle the application and to request approval of the name First National Bank of El Paso. Mr. Jones reported that another group had got in ahead of them with a request for a charter. Joshua Raynolds of Las Vegas, New Mexico, a prosperous and well known Southwestern banker, had the name they wanted and the approval of the Comptroller. The St. Louis group was disappointed and discouraged.[12]

By January of 1881 the matter was still hanging fire and Henry Newman decided to see what he personally could do about it, writing directly to the Comptroller of the Currency in Washington on Noble and Orrick's letterhead.

St. Louis Jan'y 29, 1881

Honl. Comptroller of Currency
Washington
D. C.

Sir,

In connection with the parties named herein I wish the privilege of establishing a National Bank at El Paso, Texas, with a capital of fifty thousand dollars and with the privilege of increasing the capital to one hundred thousand dollars. If we cannot have the privilege of the title of

"First National" we shall use El Paso National. We however made application through Mr. E. D. Jones . . . in October last at which time you wrote him of the difficulties in the way. We at once went to work to comply with your instructions, and addressed our letter to the Honl. Oliver Wellborn, M. C. from Texas, who at the time was absent from Washington, which caused much delay before he made for us the application, and when he did there had been another application filed. We mailed to the Honl. Oliver Wellborn on or about the fourteenth inst. a formal application as per instructions given me in yours of the 11th inst., and he telegraphs me today, Papers not yet received. It seems we are peculiarly unfortunate. I now mail to you direct and hope you may be able to grant that request and forward papers and necessary instructions to me at once at No. 3037 Washington Avenue. Mr. Wellborn says he will endorse and get the members from the El Paso district to also endorse our application. I hope as our first application was made in October, you may be able to grant us the title of First National. If not we shall use El Paso National.[13]

Why the name El Paso National was abandoned we can only guess now. One of the bank officers in our time suggests that El Paso in 1880 was so insignificant the use of its name might have done more harm than good. The final choice, by whatever means it was decided on, was The State National Bank of El Paso.

While the bank charter got nowhere, Morehead's other schemes were flourishing. By April 1 he was long gone from St. Louis and had moved his base of operations to Fort Worth, probably because he was about to go to work for the Texas and Pacific Railroad. On his trip west he had looked the situation over for the railroad officials and had reported to them on his return. Here is his description of the result:

I will here state that when I made my report to General Dodge, president of the Railroad Construction Co., giving him, according to his previous request, the general conditions at El Paso, and the country we passed over, the situation of the railroads North and Westward, the extent of the pass and the amount of supplies to be had in El Paso, he decided to begin in El Paso and grade the line eastward. The contractors about Fort Worth were afraid to undertake this work. A company was made up of Col. Hunter, H. L. Newman, Mr. Orrick and others with means and made a contract to grade 150 miles from El Paso east. These parties made an arrangement with a railroad builder to come out in charge of the active work, and with me to take charge of the business part and handle the money, the work was done. The mules and scrapers and all other outfit were purchased in Kansas City and shipped to Rincon, and from there the mules were hitched up to two horse wagons which were in demand in El Paso, and the whole outfit hauled down to the work. The contract was completed in good time, and the outfit sold out to other contractors on other roads and there was a handsome profit to the contractors.[14]

Morehead does not elaborate on just how handsome the profit was, but Owen White in his pioneer history of El Paso says that this grading contract brought the first big money to the town.[15]

Morehead undoubtedly had his business with the railroad well in hand before he left Fort Worth on his second trip to El Paso. On January 14, 1881, he was ready to make the big move. The quickest way to get there was to ride the train back to St. Louis, and this Mr. Morehead did, taking his wife and daughter with him. At St. Louis O. T. Bassett joined them and they traveled by way of Kansas City down into New Mexico on the Santa Fe, which by this time had reached San Marcial about 150 miles from their goal. They were sitting in the sleeping car in the yards at San Marcial when the porter came in to tell them that eight dead Mexicans were laid out on the depot platform, killed that very day within sight of town by Indians.

"I think you should stay in this sleeper and go on back home," Morehead said to his wife.

"I will go back if you will," she replied.

They talked it over. There was the grading contract – the bank – the new lumber yard Mr. Bassett was planning to set up. The men decided that they would have to go on, dead men or no, and Mrs. Morehead stayed with the party. They took a construction train to Rincon, fifty miles closer to El Paso, and rode the stage in from there.[16]

Meanwhile The State National Bank was showing more and more signs of life. Shortly after his arrival Morehead drew up (if he did not bring the papers with him) Articles of Association for the new firm. Copies went to St. Louis and were signed and notarized. W. H. Austin, a nephew of the Newmans who was to be the cashier, signed his copy in Fort Worth. On February 15 the El

Paso contingent signed before Adolf Krakauer, a rich man later but now glad to pick up his fee as a notary public. The Association was to function for a term of twenty years. There were to be five directors. The first meeting of stockholders was scheduled for March 23, 1881. The signed articles, as required by law, were sent off to Washington. The next move was up to the Comptroller of the Currency.

Late in January Morehead had received a letter reflecting the state of mind of the bank personnel and spotlighting his own kindness and helpfulness. It was written by the new cashier, William H. Austin — twenty-six years old, eager to further his banking career and grateful for a helping hand.

Fort Worth, Texas, Jan. 25, 1881

Dear Mr. Morehead:

I received your very kind letter this morning saying that you thought the bank a certainty, and I cannot tell you how glad it made me feel. I had been feeling anything but encouraged since we lost the charter for the First National and it was a happy surprise to know that it would be all right so soon. I cannot tell you how much I appreciate your kindness in endorsing the note and thus enabling me to carry the stock. It is but one more repetition of many kindnesses to me and I assure you, although everything has always been on one side that I never will forget it, and my only hope is that I may some day be in a condition to make you some return. Write and tell me everything about El Paso and about board and houses out there.

. . . .

I am your friend,
Wm. H. Austin.[17]

Nine years later this letter was to bring no small embarrassment to Mr. Austin, but at this moment all was well in Mr. Morehead's official family. The only thing needed to complete his happiness and satisfaction was a piece of paper signed by the Comptroller opening the bank for business.

The organizers were not the type to sit on their hands under any circumstances, and the lack of a piece of paper did not seem to them a major obstacle. They went about their duties as if they already had it. The story has been told that Mr. Morehead organized his firm and was in operation within three days of his arrival in El Paso, and the tale may be true.[18] The first stockholders' meeting was held on schedule on March 23. Colonel Hunter (one of the great names in the cattle-raising West) arrived from St. Louis with proxies in his pocket for shareholders unable to be present. H. L. Newman came with him. The list of stockholders, representing 550 shares at $100 each, was as follows:

C. R. Morehead	El Paso	100 shares
Ynocente Ochoa	El Paso	50
Joseph Magoffin	El Paso	20
Oscar T. Bassett	El Paso	30
Henry L. Newman	St. Louis	60
John C. Orrick	St. Louis	50
Robert D. Hunter	St. Louis	50
William H. Austin	El Paso	50
Sarah E. Newman	St. Louis	40
Edwin B. Sherzer	St. Louis	25
S. T. Newman	St. Louis	25
John J. O'Fallon	St. Louis	20
James C. Moore	St. Louis	10
Thomas Rankin	St. Louis	10
Augustus F. Shapleigh	St. Louis	10

By vote of these stockholders, present or represented by their proxies, five directors were named: H. L. Newman, Joseph Magoffin, O. T. Bassett, W. H. Austin, and C. R. Morehead.

The directors at their own meeting, following the election, took up as the first item of business the election of officers. To no one's surprise, these turned out to be the following: C. R. Morehead, President; Joseph Magoffin, Vice President; W. H. Austin, Cashier. Mr. Austin, as we shall see, did not remain long with the firm, but Morehead and Magoffin were to hold their offices for the next forty years.

It might be of interest to this generation to learn that the President's salary was $300 per month. The Cashier got $2,500 per year, and that was good pay in 1881.[19]

No mention was made of a business address, but the bank's first home was already completed. It was a brick building — some say the first brick business building in El Paso — on the north-east corner of El Paso and San Antonio streets, the very heart of the village. The bank did not own the property. It belonged first to Joe Brower, an immigrant from Tombstone known as the Flying Dutchman. He bought the brick from Zach White's new factory and the land from Judge Allen Blacker, whose house and lots fronted on San Antonio Street just east of the new building. By the time the structure was completed, Brower had sold the property to Major W. J. Fewel, and the bank leased from him.[20]

The headquarters of The State National Bank was eighty-five feet by twenty, the long side on El Paso Street. A door at the corner admitted clients and depositors to the business area, and a counter on the east side separated the staff from the customers. Mr. Morehead had a private door on the San Antonio Street side leading to his private office. There was a small safe somewhere, and a couple of ledgers, but that was all the equipment the bank had to start with. At first Morehead and Austin were the entire staff. It was banking reduced to bare essentials, but there it was, ready for business.

For the moment Mr. Morehead had the field to himself. The First National was not yet in operation in spite of its head start, and official approval for the State National was not long in coming. On April 23, 1881, a telegram from John J. Knox, Comptroller of the Currency, arrived by courtesy of the Army Signal Corps. It said: "Papers just received, You can commence business."[21]

The bank, as we have seen, was already born, but it was reassuring to have the birth certificate.

Chapter II

BORDER TOWN

• El Paso in 1880 was still a frontier outpost, complete with gunfights, lynchings, and Indian raids close at hand. Boom times were on the way, but in the spring of that year the town was passing through its last days of isolation and frontier individualism. Every man followed his own code and righted his own wrongs, if he had any, and a surprising number of citizens did[1]

About nine hundred people, mostly Mexicans, lived on the American side of the river. Paso del Norte, across the way, was the largest town on the Mexican border, as it still is, but its total population at that time was only four or five thousand. It had a city government but it was a tolerant community also – in some ways more tolerant than El Paso. The two centers got on well with each other. There was much international partying among the fine ladies and gentlemen of both countries.[2] On a lower level, the crooks and confidence men, of whom there were many, operated on both sides of the river, shifting their base of operations when things got too hot for comfort.

The fifty-odd Anglos who called El Paso home were a special breed. They seemed indifferent to the heat and sandstorms and monotony of their village, probably because they were all hoping for better days just ahead. Every one of them had property which he clung to through thick and thin because it would one day be valuable – might make him rich. It all depended on the railroad. Everybody lived for the day when the steel highway would arrive.[3]

It should have arrived long ago. The Texas and Pacific had reached Fort Worth in 1876 and stopped there for four long years. The Galveston, Harrisburg and San Antonio (later part of the Southern Pacific System) arrived in San Antonio in 1877. In 1880 it was still there. The panic of 1873 had brought business to a halt and money was tight for a while, but by 1880 the sap was rising once more in the economic tree and the railroad magnates prepared to move.[4]

While they reshuffled their cards in preparation for renewing the game, El Paso remained the same violent little hell hole that it had been since the Civil War. The Republicans — Union men — had lost their grip only three years before as a result of the explosion known as the Salt War of 1877, in which half a dozen men met untimely deaths.[5] In 1879 Victorio, the great Apache leader, left the Mescalero Reservation a hundred miles north of El Paso and swept through New Mexico, Old Mexico and West Texas, cutting a swath of death and destruction as he went. He circled El Paso as Texas Rangers, Mexican Rurales, the United States Army and embattled ranchmen pursued him, fell into his ambushes, and never quite caught up until the final campaign. In October, 1881, he was surrounded a hundred miles below El Paso in Chihuahua and his band wiped out or scattered.[6]

Captain George W. Baylor brought his Ranger detachment to Ysleta in 1879 and fought the last Indian fight in Texas against survivors of Victorio's band in the wild country near Guadalupe Peak in 1881.[7]

The town which was a focus for all this violence and excitement was what you would have expected in such a country. It was little; it was crude; it was short on religion, education, culture and good women.

It was a one-street community. A town had been platted in 1859 but nothing much had happened to any thoroughfare but El Paso Street, so called because its extension through the sandhills took one by a meandering route to the river, where he could ford or ferry. At the head of this street was the Plaza, the spot we now call Pioneer Plaza or the Little Plaza to distinguish it from San Jacinto Plaza a block to the east. Through this little sun-soaked square the village irrigation ditch ran, and people with something to sell gathered to display their wares. San Francisco Street entered the square from the west, and a few business houses, notably those belonging to the Schutz brothers, were functioning there. The Central Hotel looked directly south down El Paso Street. The White House department store occupies the site now. Where the Mills Building stands, Mrs. Rohman had her hotel, and directly across the way, about where the Plaza Motor Hotel rises now,

Major and Mrs. Braxton Gillock ran another hostelry. San Antonio Street and St. Louis Street were in existence and had been named for the destination of the stagecoaches which traversed them at infrequent intervals, but they were sandy trails rather than streets. Between the center of town, such as it was, and Joseph Magoffin's country place a mile or so east, there were fields and vineyards. Magoffin himself had a fine orchard, as did everybody else who owned an acre of soil. Much good farm land went to waste when El Paso became a city.[8]

The focus of interest for the males of the town was Ben Dowell's place where the Hotel Paso del Norte now rises. It was a one-story adobe saloon and clubroom where business deals, happy reunions, lynchings and gunfights were arranged, and also horse races. The race track was a straightaway running west on what is now West Overland Street.[9] Across from Dowell's establishment on the southeast corner of El Paso and San Antonio Streets was Jack Doyle's place, famous in its day, and southward for a block or two, on both sides of the way, stores and saloons and gambling halls were interspersed until the street petered out, ending in a few adobe shacks where some of the Mexican population lived.

There was no civil government. The town had organized in 1873[10] with Ben Dowell as mayor, but after 1875 the council ceased to function. Nobody wanted to pay taxes or submit to regulation, and the citizens seemed perfectly happy to live in anarchy. By 1880, however, conditions became so bad that the survival of those citizens was at stake, and in the interest of self-preservation, they elected Solomon Schutz to the Mayor's office in July of that year.

It was not really El Paso's fault that matters were going from bad to worse. Events far away were having their repercussions here in West Texas. The Santa Fe was building south from Albuquerque. The Southern Pacific was laying track toward El Paso from two directions. The rails reached Tucson on March 20, 1880, and the eastern division was well out of San Antonio by that date. The Texas and Pacific was working at full speed west of Fort Worth, reaching Baird on December 4.[11] As a result the population of El Paso began to swell perceptibly. Stage lines ran from each end-of-track and every day new faces appeared on the streets and new businesses sprang up. Typical was Elbridge A. Stuart, an Indiana boy who decided to go into business for himself in El Paso and set up a general-merchandise store in a tent on South El Paso Street before the railroads arrived. The store was a success, but the risks were almost too great for young Mr. Stuart. According to his biographer, he stepped out of his tent on one occasion and before he had walked more than three blocks, he stepped over six dead bodies of men who had been shot down on the street. He had not owned a gun up to this time, but immediately went out and bought one. He kept it for about a week. Then somebody stole it.

Assisted probably by his training in such an exacting school, Elbridge went on to found the Carnation Milk Company with its contented cows and stockholders and became a titan of American business.[12] But that came later.

Many another solid citizen of Elbridge Stuart's type came in just ahead of the railroad – men for whom schools and subdivisions and streets were later named, men who built and planned and looked to the future. It seemed, however, that the majority of the newcomers were what used to be called "sporting" people, which means that they were out to get all they could from the non-sporting citizens by pandering to their sinful impulses. For the first ten years of the boom, confidence men were a plague. Gamblers of all types, from cheap tinhorns to big-time operators in elegant white hats and Prince Albert coats, turned up in quantities. "Entertainers" stopped off to assist with the shows provided by the variety theatres.[13] In the very early eighties "Big Alice" Abbott, Gypsy Davenport and a charming redhead named Etta Clark began operating the plush parlor houses that people talked about in lands far away from the Mexican border. For years El Paso was known as the hottest town in the West. There was a saloon on every corner, often with gambling rooms in the rear or upstairs. Utah Street, now South Mesa, was the street of sin, with attractions all the way from pretentious parlor houses to lowly cribs. The Red Light and Monte Carlo dance halls were meeting places of a somewhat different kind, but just as popular.[14]

At the beginning of 1880 the free-and-easy atmosphere of the frontier was still there. If not always peaceful, it was at least relaxed. Nobody minded anybody else's business. There was room for all without crowding. Tomorrow could take care of itself. Before the year was half over, however, all this had changed. The rush of new people had begun. Rooms were not to be had and the houses, many of which had been empty a few years before, were all occupied. Adobe was there in plentiful supply, but lumber and glass and nails were almost non-existent until railroad transportation became available. Mr. Bassett's new lumber yard was open for business, but even Mr. Bassett could not sell building materials until he could get them himself.

These shortages could not slow down the tide of immigration. El Paso Street could hardly hold the newcomers. The crowd was so great, as James B. Gillett observes in *Six Years with the Texas Rangers,* that "there was not enough room for people to walk on the sidewalks and they filled the streets. . . . If one wished a seat at the gambling tables, he had to come early or he could not get within thirty feet of them."[15]

By early summer conditions were so close to getting out of hand that some sort of civic organization was absolutely necessary, and the County Court, on petition from the citizens, set up an election. On July 23, 1880, Mayor Solomon Schutz met with his new council, and the wheels of government began to turn.[16] The first ordinances were aimed at raising money (every saloon had to pay an occupation tax of ten dollars a year), but the great concern of the council was to find ways of controlling the vice and crime, violence and viciousness which were making the town a perilous place for everybody. Their luck was not good until the spring of 1881 when the famous marshal Dallas Stoudenmire began his reign. Three days after his appointment – the date was April 14, 1881 – Stoudenmire was involved in a shoot-out on El Paso Street in which four men died in less than that many minutes,[17] and after that El Paso behaved itself a little better. It remained a six-shooter town, however, until long after the turn of the century.

Law and order or no law and order, it was obvious to many people that El Paso was going to be an important place when the rails arrived, and they hurried to get in on the ground floor. Marcellus Washington Carrico came to town in April of 1880 and prepared to get out the El Paso *Times.* His counterparts Barron F. Deal and Charles Baker were not far behind him in planning for the first issue of the El Paso *Herald*. Both papers seem to have reached the street on the same day – April 2, 1881.[18] Signs of progress were visible everywhere. The Pierson Hotel, three stories tall with broad balconies going all the way around the first two floors, was rising where the home of the Newspaper Printing Corporation stands now. It opened soon after the advent of the railroad. In January the city council granted a franchise to a street railway company. In the spring the El Paso Water Company was organized. Even a gas company was chartered. The first mule car ran in 1882; water flowed (oozed might be a better word) through the water company's mains for the first time in 1883; the first gas jet was lit in 1884. Even so, the transformation of the frontier village into a small city went forward at a pace which seemed to the pioneer settlers nothing short of miraculous.

The moment for which El Paso had waited so long and which opened the door to revolutionary changes occurred on May 26, 1881. On that date the railroad actually arrived. Pigtailed Chinese workers had laid the rails into town some time before, and work trains had puffed in and out. The great event, however, was the arrival of the special train bearing C. F. Crocker, President of the Southern Pacific system, and his official party. Everything was done that could be done to make this the greatest celebration of the century. There were welcoming speeches full of resounding oratory, a banquet at the Central Hotel and a ball at Schutz's Hall, newly floored and specially decorated for this affair.

The issue of the *Herald* which describes the festivities has been preserved, leaving no doubt that this was one of the great occasions in El Paso history. Everybody who was anybody was there with his wife, and the editors joyfully described the ladies' dresses, listed the selections on the musical program played by the band from Paso del Norte at the ball, quoted the speeches as accurately as possible. Dallas Stoudenmire, the new marshal, was there in amiable mood. Joseph Magoffin, stout and smiling, appeared with his daughter on his arm. Mr. and Mrs. O. T. Bassett attended, and so did Mr. and Mrs. W. H. Austin, the latter in black silk and coral jewelry. Mrs. Morehead did not appear, but Mr. Morehead was present. The bank had been open for only a month, but already the new officers were taking their places in the community.

Chapter III

THE FIRST YEARS

• Before the civil war banks were scarce in Texas. In far West Texas, they were nonexistent. A bank in Galveston was chartered by the Congress of Coahuila and Texas just before the Mexican War, and the Banco de Comercio y Agricultura actually operated under this charter until 1858.[1] It was the only chartered bank in the state before the War. Most of the business was done by "private banks," operating as part of larger mercantile or commission firms. People who bought and sold were in the business of handling money. They necessarily had to operate an exchange business, since all sorts of currencies were afloat in the Southwest.[2] It was part of their responsibility also to transmit money for their customers by draft or letter, and in so doing they exercised some, at least, of a bank's functions. Since they were obliged to provide for the safekeeping of their own money and other assets, they frequently did the same for their customers and patrons. They bought and sold on commission and served as insurance agents; but they were bankers only incidentally.

Coin was scarce, and a surprising number of substitutes for it were in use. Almost any kind of promise to pay could be used instead of money: railroad scrip, individual and corporate notes and I.O.U.'s, paper issued by individuals and business firms. Much confusion resulted, but somehow business was carried on.

Texas was traditionally and historically suspicious of banks and of paper money issued by banks. The Constitution of 1845 outlawed both, hoping thereby to solve all future financial difficulties. The Constitution of 1866 prohibited state banks. There was no such thing in Texas until 1869, when a new constitutional convention authorized them. Immediately forty-eight state banks were chartered, although only eighteen actually opened.[3]

The Federal Banking Law of 1863 had provided for the establishment of national banks chartered by the Comptroller of the Currency, but the stipulation that each bank so chartered must have a capital of $50,000 made things difficult in Texas, where money was scarce. In 1865 and 1866 four national banks were authorized, but that was only a beginning. The needs of the state far exceeded the resources of the state and national banks actually in operation. As a result a great many new private banks came into existence, unregulated and now forgotten.

There was one in El Paso. One of our earliest pictures of the Little Plaza (probably taken in 1879) shows a sign on a wall where the Blumenthal Building now stands: BANK OF EL PASO. No record of any sort referring to this pioneer bank has turned up. The State Banking Department has records of private banks only since 1906[4] and we are not likely to learn any more than we know now about this early-day enterprise.

In 1911, however, the First National Bank decided, rather belatedly, to claim the Bank of El Paso as its own parent institution, thereby elbowing The State National Bank out of its claim to priority. The annual report of the Chamber of Commerce introduced its paragraph on the First National as follows:

> Established in the seventies, the Bank of El Paso, reorganized in 1881 as the First National Bank of El Paso, with a capital of $50,000 is the oldest Banking house within El Paso's 1200 mile trade circle.

No documentary evidence has turned up in support of this statement, and until it does, The State National Bank will continue to regard itself as the pioneer bank in El Paso.

During the years after the Civil War national banks became more and more common, though they were anything but commonplace. In 1874 there were ten of them in Texas.In 1880 there were fifteen. It was a distinction for El Paso to have one of them. It was a tremendous distinction for her to have two. On June 6, 1881, six weeks after The State National Bank was officially approved, the First National Bank received its permission to begin business[5] and opened up behind Joseph Schutz's store on San Francisco Street, where it remained until its new two-story building could be erected directly across San Antonio Street from Mr. Morehead's one-story structure. Admittedly the First National had more than an extra story. It had more money and did more business than Mr. Morehead's establishment,[6] and that was all right with Mr. Morehead. Bigness meant very little to him. Soundness meant a great deal more; and the wisdom of his view is demonstrated by the fact that his bank is still doing business. The First National fell with a resounding crash in 1931.

Undoubtedly he was cautious and conservative in making loans, but El Paso was still close to frontier times and he had to do business with some frontier characters. It is worth pointing out that the first loan approved by the Board of Directors, in the sum of $200, was to George Speck, a saloon keeper and professional gambler. It was for a term of thirty days and was endorsed by B. Schuster and Company, a highly respectable firm of merchants.[7] There was no reason why George should not have asked for and received a loan. He was in a legitimate business and the Senate Bar and Gambling Hall was probably making money.

Mr. Morehead's qualities as a banker, however, are highlighted by the fact that in 1884 George Speck had changed his banking affiliations and was in trouble. On April 18, 1884, he negotiated a loan at the First National Bank and on April 30 consolidated all his indebtedness, giving a deed of trust to the bank. In June the bank foreclosed, and everything inside the saloon was taken out in front and sold at auction—fixtures, glassware, pool-parlor furniture, even twelve steel engravings and six oil paintings. Without knowing all the facts, we can deduce that Mr. Morehead had unloaded George in time to save himself from trouble.

By this time the bank was making good progress in getting through the housekeeping chores that had been neglected at the time of organization and opening. The second annual meeting of stockholders, followed by the yearly election of officers, was held on January 15, 1882. The chief item of new business at the stockholder's meeting was the adoption of a set of by-laws. The usual matters were covered — annual meeting on the second Tuesday in January; five directors to be appointed by the stockholders; and so on. What seemed to be mostly on the minds of the management, however, was the matter of employee ethics. Everyone was required by Section 10 of the By-laws to subscribe to "the following affirmation": "I do solemnly swear that I will honestly and faithfully and impartially discharge all my duties . . . and will keep secret the business of said bank." Even the directors were warned in Section 11: "No director shall be permitted to disclose any proceedings of the Board not intended to be made public. Nor shall any director communicate to any person other than a director the manner in which any member shall have acted on any question." Mr. Morehead was not one to put up with loose talk.

These by-laws were modified from time to time as need arose. A particularly interesting section was added on January 14, 1908. It was signed by C. R. Morehead and George D. Flory and it said: "No one who makes a habit of using intoxicants or that gambles shall hold any office or position of any kind in this Bank and the directors shall be the judges of whether or not such is the case."[8]

Mr. Morehead must have had a good reason for inserting this clause. Even in 1908 the manners and customs of the frontier, so far as drinking was concerned, were still accepted in spite of several generations of reformers who had been trying to clean up the town. The matter is made still more mysterious by the fact, attested to by people with long memories, that Mr. Morehead was no rabid teetotaler himself. Occasionally he took half an hour off in the middle of the morning and walked over to the Coney Island Saloon.[9] The ruling was probably a weapon to be held in reserve in case some loose-principled young man needed to be disciplined, and Messrs. Morehead and Flory had such a young man in mind.

Another matter of major interest to the directors was the need for an adequate base of operations. They seem to have intended to get out of Major Fewel's building and into one of their own as soon as possible. The fact that the First National was moving into sumptuous and spacious new quarters may have had something to do with the decision. It must have been frustrating to the directors and officers of the State National to look across the street from their one-story rented establishment and see that second story going up for the use and profit of the rival institution. They acquired a desirable lot one block east, on the corner of San Antonio and Oregon Streets (where the bank has been ever since), and prepared to build. Ground was broken in January of 1882.[10] The work went forward at a good rate of speed, and opening day was set for September 4, 1882.[11] On that date the State National began business in a fine red-brick building which compared favorably with the one erected by the First National. It had a second story and also a covered portico to protect the front door, a feature which the First National could not match. This porch extended westward as far as the alley in order to protect the front doors of adjacent business establishments. Tenants such as doctors, lawyers and insurance companies rented space upstairs and such pioneer firms as Emerson and Berrien's furniture store and John Julian's wholesale liquor business succeeded each other on the ground floor next to the bank. In 1882 the Weather Bureau moved its office and equipment into the bank building and erected an anemometer on the roof.[12]

For its day the interior of the bank was up-to-date and attractive. Chandeliers with oil lamps lighted the lobby.[13] The wooden floors were neat if not sumptuous, and in due time they were covered with a marble mosaic. The working quarters behind the scenes were given no such expensive treatment, and in time the flooring in the tellers' cages became so badly worn that a coin dropped on the floor would sometimes continue on through a crack into the basement. When this happened, the teller had to go down and hunt for it. The tellers worked in cages of polished mahogany topped by wire screens. At the south end of this section of the bank a partition divided the floor space in half. Behind the partition the officers had their desks and Mr. Morehead had his office. The water cooler, the stairway to the basement, and the one and only lavatory were there also. The whole establishment was only twenty-four feet wide and seventy-six feet long but it managed to take care of all the bank's business for almost forty years — until it was replaced in 1921.

Behind the three tellers' cages the three bookkeepers had their high desks and their big Boston ledgers. They worked in a sort of twilight zone until electric lights – miracle of the age – became available and Mr. Morehead had them installed for the comfort and wellbeing of his employees. A naked bulb twinkled at the end of a drop cord in each of the spaces alloted to the bookkeepers, but the value of this gift of science was somewhat lessened by the fact that Mr. Morehead's Scotch constitution would allow for no more than a twenty-five watt bulb at the end of each cord. An adventurous bookkeeper once took the extreme step of buying a hundred-watt bulb and installing it in his work space, but Mr. Morehead came by, saw it, and ordered it removed. "You are not going to waste the bank's money on that!"[14] he said.

The vault was fireproof but not exactly burglar proof by present-day standards. Inside, the safe and the steel money chest were kept.[15] A safe-deposit facility was included. Patrons had to buy their own boxes, but the bank stored them without charge.[16]

Business increased slowly but steadily. Some of it undoubtedly came from the stockholders and directors. The ones who lived in El Paso were all doing very, very well. O. T. Bassett's lumber yard was coining money. Since it was the largest and best in a boom town, it could hardly do otherwise.[17] Joseph Magoffin, like other citizens with real estate to dispose of, was in good condition also. Ynocente Ochoa, a stockholder, was the most important merchant in Paso del Norte and had a store on the American side at the corner of San Francisco Street and the Little Plaza. He was growing richer by the minute and was doing his banking at The State National Bank. With so much business the original staff was beginning to be too small to take care of the extra load and at the annual meeting on March 21, 1883, J. M. Thatcher was hired at $100.00 a month to help out, probably as a bookkeeper. In 1884 he was replaced by J. A. Russell.

It is worth noting that at the 1883 meeting the proxies for the St. Louis stockholders were voted by B. A. Nebeker. In 1889 he became Morehead's son-in-law. For a good many years B. A. and his sons, Charles and Eugene, were involved in the affairs of the bank. Charles was an assistant cashier from 1919 through 1922, after which time he lived in California, as did Eugene. They continued to hold stock. Mrs. Dexter Mapel, Sr., who was Lemire (Queenie) Nebeker, daughter of B. A. Nebeker and granddaughter of C. R. Morehead, is still one of El Paso's great ladies and a major stockholder in The State National Bank.

The 1883 meeting of stockholders was not an entirely happy one. There was bad news. "It was . . . voted and carried that the loss on the raised draft on Dormell, Lawson and Simpson amounting to $2707.47 be charged to profit and loss and the balance of profit on hand, $150, be carried in undivided profits as a balance on hand."

It is easy to see that the bank was not operating on a wide margin. Nevertheless it paid good returns to the stockholders from the first. The records show that a dividend has never been missed, though the percentage has been reduced a few times in lean years. A dividend of 4% on the capital stock was declared on January 5, 1882. It went up to 4½% in July of 1882, and to 6% in July of 1883. From that time on it was usually six percent, declared twice yearly. A return of 12% on an investment is almost as wonderful and desirable as manna from heaven and helps to explain why State National Bank stock has never been easy to buy.

As the dividends continued to accumulate, the surplus increased. At the first meeting of stockholders, ten percent of net earnings was assigned to surplus — no sum mentioned. On July 8, 1882, the surplus was increased by $322.70; on July 2, 1883, $5,000 was added; on January 2, 1884, the addition was $1,500; on July 1, 1884, it soared to $6,000. After that it kept on soaring. And good things happened from time to time to make business better: for instance in September, 1883, the bank was designated a United States Depository.[18]

Meanwhile the great world of finance, of which The State National Bank of El Paso was a very small part, was having the usual ups and downs which might have been expected to have some effect on cash and credit at the Pass of the North. Times were hard in 1884, for instance. Banks in the East were seriously affected. In May four of them in New York City and one in Brooklyn closed on the same day. On the day following there were more closings.[19]

For some reason financial institutions in the West seem not to have been in much difficulty during this crisis, and the El Paso banks were hardly affected at all. The El Paso *Times* commented on June 20:

> The capital and surplus of The State National Bank is now seventy thousand dollars ($70,000). They might for the time have been more prosperous if they had taken advantage of the many opportunities to have been more exacting toward their patrons, but "live and let live" has been their motto and practice.[20]

The good opinion of the *Times* was borne out in the following year when the national bank examiner showed up one morning and began an inspection of both the El Paso banks. The *Times* reported on September 13, 1885:

> Bank Examiner Henry for this district put in an appearance day before yesterday, and quietly commenced the examination of the First National and yesterday of The State National Bank. The Examiner, having made a thorough and complete examination, pronounces these institutions to be not only sound and solid, but away above the average. This report is gratifying not only to the stockholders, but it is exceedingly so to the business community who entrust much of their wealth to the good faith and business tact of the managers of our banks. Besides this, it is a source of great pride to the City of El Paso to be able to say that as a part of the history of the past two years, so full of depression and disaster to the money institutions all over the country, ours have successfully weathered these storms and come out much stronger than they were before.

The issue of October 27 noted that other communities had not done as well. "There have been bank failures at Harrold, Wichita Falls and Henrietta a few days ago."

Even in El Paso, that favored city, there was some distress. Heavy rains stopped rail traffic from the East. There was danger of a serious food shortage, and nobody came to stay at the local hotels. The Pierson, which had not been doing well anyway, had to close down. The furniture was sold at auction on the premises and brought $5,100 – enough to cover two chattel mortgages.[21] There were other business disasters, for instance the failure of the Phoenix saloon.[22] But The State National Bank went marching on.

The year 1886 brought the bank to the end of its adolescence. Many changes had come to the town. Electric lights and gas lights were available and some businessmen who could not make up their minds had installed both. A telephone exchange was servicing over a hundred phones. The Volunteer Fire Department was speeding to fires at the summons of a six-shooter volley. Several churches and a fine schoolhouse had been operating for several years. A magnificent hotel, the Grand Central, rose where Mrs. Rohman had conducted her modest business in 1880. J. Fisher Satterthwaite, a migrant from New York, was grading streets, installing utilities and building houses in the hills north and west of the downtown section. Everybody was making money and business was excellent.

True, El Paso was not yet a center of culture and refinement. The gamblers and saloon men and good-time girls came close to outnumbering the virtuous people[23] and had plenty of influence in the town's affairs. Entertainment was plentiful, but it was not high class. The Coliseum, the Gem Theatre (behind the Gem Saloon) and the National Theatre provided variety shows and sometimes athletic events for the local sports, but the Myar Opera House, where opera and legitimate drama were to flourish, was still a year away. Law and order was maintained after a fashion, but city revenue was reinforced by "fines" imposed on prostitutes and license fees collected from gamblers. El Paso was a good-time town, "The Monte Carlo of the West," a fact which shocked and repelled a good many people but did no harm to the bankers.

The big difficulty in the banking business, as it affected The State National Bank, was a rebellion within its own ranks. Eighty years after the event it is impossible to know exactly what happened but there was trouble upstairs. Morehead and W. H. Austin, his cashier, came to a parting of the ways. Tradition in the Newman family says that H. L. Newman was involved and that he broke with Morehead.[24] Newman continued to serve on the Board of Directors of the State National through 1887, however. After that his stock was voted by proxy.

Meanwhile, undoubtedly with H. L. Newman's advice and consent, W. H. Austin had begun negotiations for the opening of a new bank. On July 7, 1886, he applied to the Comptroller of the Currency – on State National Bank stationery[25]– for a charter for the El Paso National Bank. He stayed with the State National just one month more. Mr. Morehead, on September 10, placed a notice in the *Times* couched in his usual dignified and reserved language and reading as follows:

> Mr. W. H. Austin having resigned the cashiership of The State National Bank of El Paso, Mr. James C. Lackland, formerly cashier of the Abilene National Bank of Abilene, Texas, has been duly elected cashier of this bank in his stead. Mr. Lackland has been long and favorably known to us, and we ask for him the confidence of the public. . . . We solicit the continued confidence and patronage of the people and promise the same careful and prompt attention to every detail of the banking business.
>
> Very Respectfully
>
> C. R. MOREHEAD, *President*

The El Paso National Bank opened its doors in a building on San Antonio Street directly across from the State National on January 1, 1887. The cashier was W. H. Austin. He and Mr. Morehead did not speak to each other for over two years.

Chapter IV

PROGRESS AND POLITICS

• The explosive growth of El Paso in the eighties plunged The State National Bank and its officers into a whirlpool of events which culminated in the hysteria of the municipal election of 1889 – an affair which almost ended as a Battle of the Banks.

There were three banks now, The State National, the First National, and the El Paso National, all in the same block on San Antonio Street. The El Paso National Bank (no relation to the bank which carries that name now) was chartered, as we have seen, in the fall of 1886 and opened on January 1, 1887, after some unusual financial maneuvers. The organizing genius was an incredible character named Clarence Rivers King, a New York aristocrat who refused to live up to his heritage. He studied geology at Yale and at 24 was put in charge of important government explorations in the West. In 1872 he exposed the great diamond hoax, a terrific swindle which almost came off.[1] Back in New York to finish a book about his geological findings, he met a young *Tribune* reporter named Edgar Beecher Bronson. As his middle name indicates, Bronson was a kinsman of Henry Ward Beecher, Harriet Beecher Stowe, and all the other Beechers. King liked the young man, made him his secretary, and sent him out to Nebraska and Wyoming to look after his rather extensive cattle interests. These interests were liquidated in 1886, just before the terrible winter which froze out Theodore Roosevelt and almost everybody else who stayed in business on the northern ranges.[2]

The sale was part of a scheme which King had been turning over in his mind for starting a bank in El Paso. Like Charles R. Morehead six years before, he foresaw a great future for the little town on the Mexican border and wanted to invest in it. He had been in and out of the place repeatedly in the course of trips to inspect mining properties in Mexico and knew that there was gold in those sandhills.

How W. H. Austin became involved with him has not been revealed. King undoubtedly knew the Newman brothers, Austin's uncles, as fellow cattle barons on the northern plains, and through them, or on his own initiative, became acquainted with Morehead's genial, likable cashier. When Austin applied to the Comptroller (on Morehead's bank stationery) for a charter for the El Paso National Bank, their plans had already been made. Morehead's announcement of Austin's resignation appeared in the *Times* on September 13, 1886, but by that time Austin was already far away. On September 2 he had attended a party in his honor at the Vendome Hotel and gone off for a month's trip to the East.[3] He could hardly have had anything else in mind than a reunion with King and Bronson in New York to work out final plans for the grand opening.

Records of the El Paso National Bank are not available, if they exist, but Austin's application lists paid-in stockholders as follows: Austin, the cashier-to-be, owned fifty shares. Edgar Bronson, president, had two hundred. William S. Hills, pioneer builder and developer, was down for 250; George B. Zimpelman, banker of Austin and Manor, Texas, for 110.[4] The major stockholder was Clarence King with 710. Their joint financial stake was $75,000. By the time the bank was ready to open on January 1, 1887, other investors had come in, including Charles Eddy, the railroad builder, who accepted the post of vice-president. The capitalization was now $150,000. F. B. Brown, H. J. Smith, W. F. Coffin, George H. Tew and W. H. Long were elected to serve with the top officers as directors. A subsidiary enterprise, the Bank of Juarez, was organized a year or so later with Max Muller in charge to buy Mexican silver and handle international business.

The El Paso National Bank was housed directly across San Antonio Street from the State National, but proximity did not breed amity. Austin seems to have been on good terms with Jim Lackland, the State National's cashier, but the feeling between Austin and Morehead was extremely bitter. In September of 1887 there was a crisis. All we know of it is a sentence written by Morehead for the El Paso *Times* of June 5, 1890: "The *Quid Nunc*, a paper published by himself [Austin] and others in September, 1887, the people are familiar with and the controversy over that between his friends and mine need not be particularized here."

The tension between Morehead and Austin was the result of personal differences. There was no personal feud involved in the rivalry between Morehead and the top men in the First National Bank, but political disagreements did just as well. Morehead and Magoffin were Democrats — old-line, conservative Democrats. Down the street at the First National, Cashier Thatcher and directors James P. Hague and Adolf Krakauer were Republicans, and liberal Republicans at that. Sooner or later there was going to be a clash.

James P. Hague was the spark plug for the Republicans. A brilliant lawyer, an effective speaker, and a good strategist, he had come to El Paso in 1870 at the age of only twenty-one to be District Judge. As a powerful member of the city council, he had kept Mayor Magoffin's seat hot from 1881 to 1885.[5] Magoffin, a portly, full-bearded, rather solemn fellow, was no such political acrobat as Hague, but as mayor and perennial alderman he did very well in the days when the formula for governing the city was a live-and-let-live arrangement with the gamblers and saloonkeepers. On the frontier reformers were few and far between and nobody thought saloons, gambling houses and prostitution could — or should — be eliminated as long as a sizable portion of the city's revenues came from the tenderloin. The thing to do was keep a tight rein on the sin merchants and see that regular collections were made from them. Mr. Morehead — like Joseph Magoffin a product of the frontier — never doubted that this philosophy was the correct one. Mr. Morehead was the unofficial boss of the town from the early eighties for something like twenty-five years and his way of thinking was the dominant one until the reformers gained enough strength to take charge. But that came much later.

In the eighties and nineties the little banker ruled from his catch-all of an office in the bank, and the threads of his authority and influence extended into every corner of town. Like a benevolent spider he preferred staying in his web to coming out of his hole to follow up these threads, but he twitched them from his stronghold and things happened at the other end. The fact that he controlled one of the three banks was a major reason for his influence. But even more important was his very real devotion to the best interests of the community.

He is called the Father of El Paso's Public Schools and he deserves the title.[6] He served on the School Board for many years, sometimes as its chairman. The old Central School, our first, was born largely as a result of his efforts, and there was never a time during his active years when he was not working and planning for the good of the system. The system has shown its gratitude by making sure that one of its units always bears his name. When the old Morehead School was torn down in 1966 after years of service, the newest, finest grade school, now functioning along the Mesa Highway, was called Morehead School.

Second only to the welfare of the schools in his mind was the need for an adequate supply of good water for his city. No cause was ever closer to any man's heart and for twenty-five years he never lost an opportunity to work and agitate and propagandize for it.

At first El Paso was slow to get excited about the water supply. It was always possible to make out a little longer with the old inadequate arrangements. What Morehead proposed was radical and expensive, and the voters always put off what had to be done eventually.

At first drinking water — the small amount that was consumed — came out of the river. Lydia Spencer Lane in her charming book *I Married a Soldier* tells how it was prepared for human use:

> The water we used . . . was brought fresh every morning from the muddy Rio Grande, and emptied into barrels for the purpose. It was of the color of rich chocolate. To settle enough for drinking, it was poured into large, porous earthen jars holding several gallons each. By degrees the impurities sank to the bottom of the jar, and the water oozed through it, keeping the contents quite cool.[7]

In very early days the irrigation ditch, which followed San Francisco Street, bisected Pioneer Plaza and wandered off toward Joseph Magoffin's orchard a mile and a half away, was the only source of water for household as well as for agricultural use. Hence one of the first acts of the City Council when it was reorganized in 1880 was to make it illegal under severe penalties "to bathe in any acequia in this city or to cast offal, filth, or impurities of any kind therein . . . or to drive any herds of sheep, goats, cattle, hogs, or other animals into any acequia within the city. . . ."[8]

As the town grew, the water in the river became less and less inviting as an adjunct to diet and people came to depend more and more on other sources of supply. After railroad service was a reality, almost everybody drank water imported in tank cars from Deming, New Mexico. Some people sank wells and imbibed the brackish liquid that emerged from their pumps. Others conscientiously avoided water entirely as a health hazard and drank nothing but whiskey.

It seemed that a real solution to the problem had been found in 1882 when Sylvester Watts of St. Louis applied for and received a franchise to go into business as the El Paso Water Company. He sent his nephews James J. and William H. Watts to take charge of the project and the result was our first water works. Two wells sunk in the bed of the Rio Grande provided the raw material. It was pumped to a big reservoir on top of the highest hill in Sunset Heights and distributed through sheet-metal mains by gravity. The city contracted to lease twenty-five hydrants at $100 per hydrant per annum.[9] The system was tested and accepted in September, 1882.[10]

There was trouble from the start. The mains would not stand pressure. If the river went dry, so did the water works. When the floods came, the fluid which went through the mains was sometimes almost too muddy to move. For a long time the town expanded far faster than the El Paso Water Company, and there was perennial agitation to get rid of it, or replace it, or have the city take it over.

S. H. Newman of the *Lone Star* was the number-one critic of the Water Company and the "old stove pipes"[11] that it used for water mains, but in 1886 the city council decided that something stronger than criticism was needed. Councilman Loomis moved that the city cancel its agreement with Sylvester Watts and either buy out his company or hire somebody else to take over. Action was postponed and the proposal came to nothing, but the *Times* was all for cancellation. The water in the mains during the first week in September, said the editor, "has been of the consistency of molasses." Barbers were unable to offer baths to the public because a patron got out of the tub in worse shape than when he got in.[12]

Mr. Morehead and many other responsible citizens were convinced that the water works ought to belong to the citizens. Eventually they came to the conclusion that the only way to get pure water was to drill wells on the mesa, the high land above the river valley near the present site of Fort Bliss. "Pure Mesa Water" was a slogan and a rallying cry in many an election. Mr. Morehead's devotion to the cause was one of the few things that could jar him loose from his command post in The State National Bank and send him into active participation in the political warfare which rent the community beginning in the late eighties. His first such venture came in 1889.

Up to this time the town had been singularly unaffected by party considerations. There was plenty of political cleavage, but people did not line up as Democrats or Republicans.[13] The fact is, there were very few Republicans to get in line, and the Democrats had to choose up sides in order to have a contest. The good old Mexican ways persisted. *Patrones* — bosses — who could control a block of votes were the key political figures. It did not much matter where the votes came from and as a matter of fact a great many of them came from Juarez. The going rate was two dollars a vote. Henchmen of the political leaders would go out the day before an election, a bag of silver dollars in the buggy, and gather up available voters — up the Valley, down the Valley, in Mexico — and bring them to a prearranged place where they would be given food, drink, and sometimes entertainment. They would be held through the night and marched to the polls next morning.[14] Both sides did it, and when the party with the most money won, the losers always screamed Fraud and Corruption.

Mr. Morehead accepted life as he found it, and the story is still heard that in moments of emergency he would fill a sack with silver dollars in the paying teller's cage at the bank and go forth to put those dollars to political use. This story remains undocumented.

Until 1887 Democratic Lions lay down with Republican Lambs and partisan hatred was a rarity. A change had begun, however. More and more Republicans had arrived as the population grew, and the Presidential campaign of 1888 brought them out in full cry for the first time since the seventies under the leadership of James P. Hague. His party was, for the time being, the advocate of reform and the foe of organized vice – the first group to call for a cleanup in El Paso.

This was a challenge to Mr. Morehead and the Democrats – conservatives who tolerated, if they did not encourage, the gamblers and saloonkeepers. Hague called the group "The Morehead Bank Gang"[15] and insinuated that the money and prestige of The State National Bank was what kept them in power and office. It was the beginning of a rift which was to grow wider as the years went by. The major issue was whether El Paso should or should not continue to be the Monte Carlo of the United States. At first the Republicans were the Law and Order Party but later on the Democrats split up into factions and fought each other over the question. Mr. Morehead always wished he could limit the issues to just one: Pure Mesa Water. But he was always having to fight on ground chosen by his opponents. More and more they insisted on discussing vice and sin.

The fall of 1888 saw the rift between Republicans and Democrats widen into a serious breach. Republicans all over the country were on the rise and the party members in El Paso County caught fire. The two newspapers took sides and began blasting each other. The *Herald* was for the Republicans and the *Times*—with much heavier artillery – supported the Democrats. Juan Hart, the *Times* editor, seemed to have an edge in handling smears and sneers, but he could not turn the tide. Harrison went in as President. The Republicans staged a great torch-light parade on the tenth of November climaxed by a delirious rally at the Myar Opera House[16] and never doubted that this was only the beginning of their triumphs.

The municipal elections the next spring provided the arena for a showdown. Waters Davis, president of the Republican club, called for a mass meeting on March 4, 1889. The Democrats assembled on March 12. A few days later both groups conducted primaries for the first time in El Paso's history. For mayor the

Republicans nominated Adolf Krakauer, a small, frail, but extremely capable Jewish merchant who was already prosperous and would soon be the richest man in town. He was universally respected and would be a hard man to beat. Since he was a director of the First National, he took the first step toward bringing the banks into collision. Morehead took the second.

The Democrats realized that the situation was serious and that they would have to put their best man in the field. There could be no question as to who he was and they proposed to Morehead that he be their candidate. Morehead refused positively with something like horror.[17]

The day came for the primary elections and still the Democrats called for Morehead. Joseph Magoffin had stepped aside in favor of his friend. The top men in the community had stated in print that nobody else would do. Morehead still said no. When the afternoon session was called to order, Captain Beall placed Morehead's name in nomination as the assembly cheered and whooped. Morehead came forward and reminded them that he had made a public announcement of his inability to serve. He suggested the name of Charles Davis. The crowd would not listen. They nominated him by acclamation "amid the wildest scene of enthusiasm." Once more he said he "must and would decline." A recess was declared while everybody present gathered around the little banker and pleaded with him to change his mind.

The climax came when W. H. Austin stepped forward, took Morehead by the hand and said, "I will take my coat off and go to work for you if you will run."[18]

It was a great moment and it brought the *Times* reporter close to tears. Since 1886, when Austin left the State National to become cashier of the El Paso National, the two men had not been speaking.

Everybody present knew all about this feud, and Austin's generous action at first left them all speechless. The *Times* reporter gave voice to the deep emotion which the entire assembly felt:

> As those two noble men — the peers of any citizen in Texas — who had been former bosom friends, but had of late years drifted so far apart as not to speak to each other, as they stood there with clasped hands, it was a picture of patriotism more than Spartan.

Not even Morehead could resist the drama and passion of such a moment. He agreed to accept the nomination and run for mayor.

It was no surprise to anybody when he announced his platform that his first thought was the new city charter which would have to be put into operation by the administration. His second was for the water question. "It is a thing of the first importance to all classes of citizens," he said, "to have pure water, cheap water, and plenty of it." It would be necessary for the city to take over the water supply, at the same time dealing "justly and liberally" with the water company.[19]

The campaign was a bitter one. Neither Morehead nor Krakauer wanted it to be that way and said so,[20] but circumstances were too much for them. El Paso's first venture into party politics generated more heat than any argument since the Salt War. The story is still told that dairymen would not deliver milk to patrons whose politics differed from their own. The newspapers hurled mud in every direction. Each side accused the other of disgraceful and immoral conduct and stepped up their charges as the tempo of campaigning rose. The Democrats said they could prove that Krakauer had voted to enfranchise the Street Railway Company in exchange for a block of stock.[21] At the same time they were making Mr. Morehead look good by going back to his record as Mayor of Leavenworth in 1869. People who had worked with him in those days sent letters of commendation and the *Times* reproduced an article from the *Leavenworth Commercial* printed in 1870 on the occasion of Mr. Morehead's retirement from the Mayor's office. It gave him credit for relieving the city of debt, placing it on a sound financial footing, building up police and fire departments, and improving streets. "He has . . . infused new life in every department, systematized the workings of each and all of them, and left the city in just such condition as we might expect from a careful, judicious business man."[22]

The *Herald* did not try very hard to rebut this and other articles run by the *Times*. It did send a man up to Leavenworth who succeeded, without too much trouble, in finding a citizen willing to affirm that Morehead had used the mayor's office for his own profit. This story was held back till the afternoon before the election. The next morning the *Times* stormed onto the street with headlines declaring that the report was "fraud and filth" and accusing the informant of being a liar and even a murderer.[23]

It was too late. Krakauer had won 892 to 855. The number of votes cast exceeded the number of qualified voters by several hundred.

The Democrats, however, refused to concede. The word had gone round before the election that Krakauer was not an American citizen, and S. H. Newman challenged him at the polls.[24] Krakauer was highly indignant at the suggestion and proceeded to cast his ballot. The Democrats were not convinced and demanded an investigation, addressing a petition to the council. The Republican members of the council, led by Alderman Hague, put off a decision as long as possible, but an inquiry was approved on April 17.[25]

At this point Mayor Lightbody, a haberdasher by trade and a hater of political red tape, decided to take matters into his own hands. He canvassed the votes with the help of the Republican Aldermen (the Democrats walked out) and installed the entire slate of officers on April 18. His action almost led to open war. The Republicans stocked City Hall with weapons and provisions, apparently convinced that the Democrats would do so if they didn't, and prepared to stand a siege. The Democrats thought some of making a battle of it, but decided to send Sheriff Jim White with an injunction. White knocked on the fortress door, informed the inmates that the law said they had to get out, and watched them decamp meekly, leaving rifles and provisions. Immediately the Democrats walked in and slammed the door. Having the upper hand, at least for the moment, they appointed G. E. Hubbard as acting mayor and continued to investigate Krakauer.[26]

It turned out that he did not have his final citizenship papers and had never been eligible to run. He was not even eligible to hold his directorship in the First National. A director had to be a citizen.

It was at this moment that the controversy threatened to become a battle of the banks. Away back in March there had been ominous rumblings. Somebody began talking about Mr. Morehead as a BANKER, using the word as if it were obscene. The *Times* picked it up: "Some people seem to think there is an offense in being a banker and with this belief they hurl the title at Mr. Morehead, forgetting their own candidate for mayor is likewise a banker."[27] No more was heard, or at least got into print, until after election, when the *Times* editor, flushed with victory, wrote an editorial titled "Banking and Politics" in which he jumped on the First National and its officers for backing Krakauer, "the little foreigner." The First National's cashier H. S. Kaufman, feeling with some justification that this was kicking a man when he was down, resolved to do what he could to get even. He went among the Republican businessmen proposing that they boycott the *Times* – a move which might well have been a death blow to the paper if properly carried out.

Editor Hart realized this and reacted violently: "Thus the bank took up the quarrel of its director, Krakauer, and served notice that it proposed to punish those who opposed its silly little man. . . . Boycotting is a very bad policy for the bank to pursue."[28]

The tug-of-war went on for two weeks and threatened to draw in titans of finance in other communities. On June 18 the *Times* accused Joshua Raynolds of Las Vegas, founder and chief stockholder in the First National, of threatening to use his five banks to "punish those who differ personally or politically with him." After this exchange of blows the principals retired to their corners and apparently did not approach the center of the ring again.

Chapter V

THE SECOND DECADE

• Ten years after Morehead and Bassett scrambled down from their spring-wagon stagecoach on February 12, 1880, the seeds they planted had produced a fine, flourishing crop. Bassett's lumber yard was prospering, a branch was making money in Douglas, Arizona, office buildings in Oklahoma City and a ranch in California were doing likewise, and the orphan boy from Vermont was about to become one of the richest men in West Texas. He and Morehead had acquired a great deal of El Paso real estate, and the bank they founded had expanded with the town. Not too rapidly, however! In 1881, when The State National Bank issued its first Statement of Condition, its total resources added up to $190,295.51. On December 19, 1890, they totaled $437,983.93. The First National Bank on the same date presented a figure of $408,433.99; the El Paso National, $672,222.77.[1] Mr. Morehead was exactly where he liked to be – neither first nor last but comfortably and safely in the middle.

The management likewise was the way he wanted it. Every year at the annual meeting in January the stockholders elected five directors who always included Morehead, Magoffin, and J. C. Lackland, the cashier. O. T. Bassett served as a director until 1888 and then left the board, probably because he disliked going to meetings. In 1890 the directors included, besides the Big Three, J. H. Russell (the assistant cashier) and B. A. Nebeker, Morehead's son-in-law. At the directors' meeting which by custom followed the stockholders' meeting C. R. Morehead was elected president; Joseph Magoffin, vice-president; J. C. Lackland, cashier; and J. H. Russell, assistant cashier.[2] This routine was followed year after year. It must have been a comfort to Mr. Morehead to know that there would be no surprises.

The St. Louis investors still held their stock, though some of the original group were gone and the division of their estates had increased the number of St. Louis stockholders. Each year their votes were cast by proxy. It was possible in those days to secure proxies without time limit, and this Mr. Morehead had arranged for soon after his bank was organized. Somebody else voted these proxies — H. L. Newman for a while, John Julian (who ran a wholesale liquor business next door to the bank), or B. A. Nebeker — but Mr. Morehead called the shots.

These were his best days. He was in full health and vigor. Through the nineties he continued to be the "strongest man" in his community financially and politically. The town suited him and he suited the town, and although the tides of change were already rising around him, he resisted them successfully for fifteen years more.

Every morning he rode the mule car — or walked — from his house on Myrtle Avenue to his bank,[3] arriving usually before anyone else got there. He was the soul of order and regularity — a cautious and careful little Scotsman, dignified and reserved and anxious to avoid public notice but keenly aware of everything that went on in his town. As much as any man he was responsible for its progress in those years of change and transition.

The population was 10,838 in 1890. If you were a visitor, you called El Paso a large town. If you were a resident, you spoke of it as a city. The streets were still ankle deep in sand most of the time — ankle deep in mud occasionally. The summer heat sent most of the well-to-do, including Mr. Morehead and his family, off to California. People who wanted to get from one place to another drove horses or rode bicycles and there was a mounting chorus of complaint about "blind bike fiends" and reckless youths who drove their buggies too fast and frightened old ladies in the residential sections,[4] but El Paso was beginning to evolve out of its horse-and-buggy period.

A good many refinements had been added to life on the border — signs of progress and change. The Social Club sponsored elegant balls, often in the district courtroom in the new courthouse, which were attended by the best society on both sides of the border in full evening dress. Shakesperean actors, operatic stars, and entertainers of all sorts on their way to or from the West Coast appeared at the Myar Opera House, El Paso's pride since 1887. Local talent was not neglected. Chopin Music Hall, across from the courthouse, was a center of musical culture. Professor Ferdinand Dewey of Boston, a fine pianist and teacher, brought important artists to its stage and sometimes performed there himself with the assistance of such talented young people as Miss Kate Moore and Miss Marie Shelton.[5]

The organization which attracted the most popular support and enthusiastic participation was the McGinty Club. Named for a song popular at the time ("Down went McGinty"), it was an elaborately casual social and musical organization with as many as three hundred members in its best days. It sponsored a fine band, a string orchestra, a mandolin club, a number of singing groups, and even a Chinese ensemble which played "weirdly charming" airs. Included also were a couple of marching organizations, a "pyrotechnical" squad, and several artillerymen who serviced the two McGinty cannon. The avowed purpose of the McGintys was to "put down liquor." Beer was their favorite beverage and they put down so much of it that a special oversize stemmed beer glass in use along the Rio Grande is still known as a McGinty.[6]

The rise of culture, it must be admitted, did not have much effect on the shady side of El Paso life. Etta Clark, the red-headed madam, occupied a palatial new thirty-two-room mansion at the corner of Utah and Second Street. An admirer of hers in the wholesale liquor business erected it for her in 1889 at a cost of $75,000. The deal also cost him his wife.[7] Saloons and gambling halls still flourished. And pistols were still used to settle differences between gentlemen. Since the police force was efficient and vice was under strict control, El Paso was not exactly a wide-open town, but it was certainly standing ajar. According to Owen White, our first historian, the reason for the order in El Paso's disorderly businesses was Mr. Morehead.

"He was the boss of El Paso," Owen declares, "and as political control of the town was then entirely in the hands of the vice element, he was looked upon by those who wanted to reform our fair city as a very vile and wicked old gentlemen. He wasn't. He was simply a wise and wily frontiersman who had had his eyeteeth cut for him in 'bleeding Kansas' and knew exactly how to handle tough men, tough women, and tough towns. . . . There wasn't a gambler, a saloon keeper, a dance-hall proprietor, not even a lady of ill-fame in the town who didn't know that any time he wanted to, C. R. Morehead could put them out of business. Therefore they had a great respect for him, and co-operated in keeping El Paso's vice industry on a level that was high indeed in comparison with any other frontier town."[8]

Owen probably overestimates the might of Mr. Morehead's arm in these matters. That he had much influence there can be no doubt. He involved himself in everything that affected the town. He had a finger in every ambitious business venture and controlled a good deal of El Paso's working capital. He believed, as we have seen, that sin is here to stay and that it ought to pay its way. There were a number of powerful men in town, however, who often opposed and sometimes defeated him.

One thing in particular was out of his control, and out of the hands of the police force and the Rangers as well for some time. This was the organized thievery and terrorism perpetrated by a group of outlaws known as the Bosque Gang. Probably "Gang" should be plural. Above town in the neighborhood of Canutillo was a *bosque* or tangled thicket where one group hung out. Below town a bigger mob holed up in another *bosque* on what was known as The Island because the old river bed ran to the east of it and the new river bed ran to the west. In wet weather it was surrounded by water. The international boundary passed through, lost in the brush, but nobody paid any attention to it. The Bosque gangs traveled back and forth through the thickets, passing east of town on the mesa where Fort Bliss stands now, and most of the way they could keep out of sight in the brush.[9] Smuggler's Pass, where the new transmountain highway runs, was so called because they would pick up cattle and horses on the east side of Mount Franklin, drive them through the gap to a corral high up on the west slope, and dispose of them when the coast was clear.[10]

On April 18, 1890, Charles Fusselman, a Texas Ranger from

Presidio with time on his hands, joined a posse chasing a gang of horse thieves toward the pass. The pursuers rode into an ambush and Fusselman died on the spot with a bullet through his neck.[11] The rocky defile leading to the crest is still called Fusselman Canyon in his memory. The Bosque gangs were not broken up until 1893 and Fusselman's murderer was not hanged until 1900.[12]

El Paso was still untamed, and would continue to be so for a good many years, but many other important issues were occupying the minds of the citizens in the crucial year of 1890. In all of them the officers, stockholders and friends of The State National Bank played major roles. It was a time of strong rivalries and deep animosities during which men tended to form tight little units like the warrior bands around a tribal chieftain. Churches, lodges and saloons brought people with common interests together, and at election time Democrats and Republicans developed ties stronger than blood brotherhood, but there were other attachments just as binding. The banks, for instance, commanded about as much loyalty as the lodges and churches. W. H. Austin, a powerful and aggressive leader, had a good portion of the town with him, whatever the issue. C. R. Morehead, though his blood pressure never got as high as Austin's, had a following just as devoted. Austin and his supporters acknowledged this to be a fact by calling Morehead and his friends "The Morehead Gang," or "The State National Bank Gang," or just "The Gang." The history of The State National Bank through this period thus becomes the history of the involvement of its officers, particularly Mr. Morehead, in civic affairs.

One of the major projects in 1890 was the International Dam which all El Paso hoped would be built just above town, providing recreation, flood control, and water for irrigating crops in both the United State and Mexico. If this dream had been realized, we might all be water-skiing and bass fishing every afternoon in the summer, but the government decided to build the dam a hundred miles north in New Mexico and completed the Elephant Butte project in 1916.[13]

A dream that *was* realized was the relocation of Fort Bliss, a matter of great importance to the El Paso banks since it would bring much new money into the community. The old post at Hart's

Mill had outlived its usefulness.[14] The Santa Fe Railway tracks bisected the parade ground, for one thing. For another, the government decided in 1889 to set up several large permanent posts on the Mexican border. There was no reason why one of them should not be located at El Paso, but such benefits, as El Paso well knew, are often lost by default. A strong effort would have to be made to present the town's case to the government. The group which undertook to carry the ball seems to have assembled spontaneously and without any publicity whatever. It consisted of two men from the El Paso National Bank group – E. B. Bronson and W. S. Hills; two from The State National Bank – Joseph Magoffin and B. H. Davis; and one – W. S. McCutcheon – who probably had ties with the First National. There can hardly be any doubt that they were behind the campaign which began in Washington in January, 1890, to bring the new post to El Paso. Senator Reagan and Congressman Lanham began to push legislation authorizing sale of the old post and application of the proceeds to purchase of a site larger than the outgrown thirty acres at Hart's Mill. On March 1, 1890, the new post was authorized and $150,000 was appropriated for construction.[15] A year later the amount was doubled.

The 1890 bill contained one clause which raised the eyebrows of people who read about it in the El Paso papers. It said that a thousand-acre site would be donated by the people of El Paso, and that it would be paid for by public subscription. For a few days everybody in town wondered who had been so generous with their money. Then the facts came out. The group headed by Joseph Magoffin had assured the House Committee on Military Affairs that they were "authorized to say that whenever the government shall determine to enlarge the post and remove it to a more favorable location, land will be donated to the government for that purpose in such quantity and at such points as the government may decide.[16]

Who had "authorized" them to make this promise they did not reveal, but it seems likely that the officers of the three banks had circulated among the leading citizens, got favorable answers, and knew what they were doing.

The committee might as well have called themselves the El Paso Chamber of Commerce. When in April they came out into the open and organized as the El Paso Progressive Association,[17] they described their objectives as follows: "To encourage immigration and the development of the manufacturing, mining, agricultural and stock growing interests of this section." Officers were elected on June 3 (Joseph Magoffin was chairman), and the most pressing business facing them was declared to be "the new military post."[18]

By this time word had come from San Antonio that General D. S. Stanley would arrive shortly to select a site, and the mayor appointed a Post Committee to confer with him. Again The State National Bank in the person of its vice president was represented. Joseph Magoffin, wearing his other hat (he was an alderman), was on this committee too.[19] The general, with a staff consisting of Lieutenant-Colonel J. C. Baily, M.D., and Lieutenant-Colonel G. N. Weeks, QMC.,[20] spent five days in El Paso considering the possibilities. Before he left on July 23, he had designated 1000 acres on the mesa northeast of town – the present location of Fort Bliss – as the only "fit and proper" place for the new garrison.[21]

The next move was up to El Paso. General Stanley had announced that construction could begin as soon as land and an assured water supply were available. A campaign to raise the required $9,000 got under way and S. W. Russell, secretary of the Military Post Committee, sent off to Fort Worth for a well borer.

At this point a number of citizens were rudely shocked to learn that The State National Bank group owned a good deal of the land to be acquired. There was some grumbling, and some questioning of Mr. Morehead's ethics by people outside the Morehead orbit. The opposition quieted down, however, when certain additional facts were made public. The key tract in the site, without which the government would reject the whole transaction, consisted of 176 acres owned by Morehead, Charles Davis, B. D. Russell, and J. T. Beall – all loyal State National Bank friends. They were naturally uneasy about the looks of the situation and eager to reassure the public. Morehead was so anxious to avoid charges of profiteering that he and his associates came before the Progressive Association and asked to have the land appraised.

The price fixed for their property was twenty-five dollars an acre. B. D. Russell, who owned a whole section in his own right, got five dollars an acre. A third tract comprising approximately 600 acres brought a lump sum of $1150. The explanation for this differential was that the holdings of the Morehead group were more valuable than the others and that land which still belonged to them would be cut off and rendered less desirable. Bronson himself, who was not likely to vote for anything that helped Morehead make money, stated for publication that at twenty-five dollars an acre the land was "cheap."[22]

Even with this explanation El Paso's doubts were not completely satisfied, and the public subscription went forward at a snail's pace. In August it still was not all in. To make matters worse, a certain Dr. Edward Alexander of Juarez declared himself to be the heir to the Ruelas Grant, going back to Spanish times, which included part of the Fort Bliss site. He said he was not about to abandon his claim when a "private individual" was trying to make "the good people of El Paso pay him $25 per acre."[23]

There was no way out of this entanglement for Mr. Morehead but to abandon his cherished anonymity and reveal that he and Charles Davis had contributed $1,000 of their own money toward purchase of the land.[24] The $3,400 they actually received from the sale of their tract to the Association they placed in escrow until the United States Court could rule on the validity of Dr. Alexander's claim. That done, Alexander executed a quit-claim deed and the way was clear for construction to begin.

The most encouraging feature of the negotiations involved the water supply. The well driller found a vein at 217 feet and another a little deeper. On August 14, with Joseph Magoffin and S. W. Russell looking on, the pumps were started. They ran for twenty-three hours, pumped 15,000 gallons of water, and were flowing as strongly at the end of the test as at the beginning. After this there could be no reason for delay. By now the money had all been raised. The government had a deed to the property. Captain George Ruhlen, in charge of construction, put his men to work and kept them at it. The troops moved in in October, 1893.

The discovery of a good water supply beneath the fort was welcome news for all the people who had joined Mr. Morehead in demanding "pure Mesa water." It was certain now that the fluid was there. If the supply could be tapped and made available, the days of river water, with its constant threat of typhoid, would be a thing of the past.

The new wells were brought into production at a time when the water question was threatening to break up the town. The two things that all the citizens of El Paso had in common were a taste for *chile colorado* and a conviction that something had to be done about the water works. S. H. Newman of the *Lone Star* had some of his finest moments speaking evil of the water company until his paper folded in 1886. After that Juan Hart of the *Times* began blasting the company and its muddy product.[25] Hart realized that Mr. Watts' system could never catch up with the demand in a rapidly expanding community. The only solution was municipal ownership; and the way to municipal ownership was through a bond issue big enough to buy Mr. Watts out.

Thanks to the efforts of Hart and other dedicated people, a bond issue was approved in 1889. The amount was $25,000. The money was to be used to locate artesian wells. Satisfactory bids were received, but the El Paso Water Company, fighting for its life, found a way to sabotage the bond issue. Sylvester Watts applied in federal court for an injunction on the grounds that El Paso had not yet reached a population level of 10,000. According to State law, only communities over 10,000 could issue bonds.

El Paso was outraged. Everybody knew that the population was well over the 10,000 mark. As soon as the census figures for 1890 were released, the world would know it too. But until those figures became available, Mr. Watts could press for his injunction. As a result of his trouble making, the prospective purchasers for the bonds became alarmed and withdrew their bids.

Convinced that the injunction was eventually doomed to defeat, the city decided to go ahead anyway and sink a test well. The question was — where to sink it? Several people, including Mr. Austin of the El Paso National Bank, offered sites, but the council was not willing to go ahead without expert advice. A government geologist named Professor Robert Hay was called in and on May 27, accompanied by three aldermen and real-estate developer W. S. Hills, he made a survey of the territory around the point of Mount

Franklin. The tour concluded, he offered some sage advice. It would be a mistake to drill on the mesa east of town, he said, or in the neighborhood of the river. The well should be sunk somewhere "between the mesa and the quicksand formation of the valley."

This was a blow to the Pure Mesa Water advocates, but they went along with the majority, who seemed to feel that if the drillers just went deep enough, they would get an artesian flow far surpassing the wells in the Pecos Valley. New bids on the water bonds were called for and the council drew up specifications for the test well, following Professor Hay's advice.

Sylvester Watts won this round also. Since his suit was still pending, he was able to convince prospective bond buyers that they had better wait a while.

At this point Mr. Morehead interposed with reassuring words. "There will be no difficulty," he said, "in placing the bonds if our large property owners will come forward and agree to carry them until the question of their legality is settled. I will take my share and The State National Bank will also take some bonds."

The El Paso National was not to be outdone. "We will do as much and take as many bonds," declared Mr. Austin, "as any other bank."[26] Nevertheless the bonds remained unsold. The banks were as unwilling as private individuals to make a premature move. And when on December 18 the Supreme Court announced that it would take about three years to get to the El Paso Water Case on account of a crowded docket, artesian water became a dead issue.

El Paso was not through trying, however. A second bond issue had already been proposed through which money would be raised for three worthwhile projects. The issue was to be for $125,000 this time — $30,000 for expansion of the public-school system, $20,000 for paying off the city's debts, and $75,000 for purchase or construction of an adequate water system. January 7, 1890, was designated as the day of decision.

It seemed impossible that the bonds should fail. One indignant citizen was quoted as saying, "My water, something which God intended should be free as air, is costing me as much as I pay for bread. . . . I pay as much for water for use in my home as I pay for bread for my little family of five."[27]

The officials of The State National Bank spoke up, as usual, for what seemed in the public interest. "I shall vote for the issuance of the bonds," said Joseph Magoffin." Mr. Morehead added, "I'm certainly in favor of the issuance of the bonds. I shall vote for every proposition submitted. . . ."[28]

To the surprise of all concerned, the bond issue was defeated. Apparently people were so sure it would pass that they felt it unnecessary to vote. Out of 537 qualified taxpayers 166 turned out. Only twenty-nine of them voted in opposition, but since the total vote cast did not amount to the required two-thirds of the eligible voters, the bonds were defeated.

A petition to resubmit was immediately circulated and a new election was held on February 21. This time the bonds were approved, but somebody had added a weasel-worded clause applying to the water bonds. It said they could not be issued until a new water works had been completed or the old one purchased. Somehow the crafty Sylvester Watts, always resourceful, must have been involved in this maneuver. If he wasn't, he was certainly delighted to hear of it.

The next setback suffered by Mr. Morehead and his Pure Water group was definitely of Mr. Watts' manufacture. It developed that $75,000 would not buy his plant, even if the city could pay it. Not long before, he had voluntarily raised the valuation to $77,000 – a fine case of business foresight.[29] Now, to make certain he was safe, he offered to sell out if the city would assume water-company debts amounting to $80,000.[30] That did the business for him. The council decided that El Paso could and would get along with river water for a while longer. The water problem continued to agitate the town, however, for a good many years.

The school bonds and the municipal-indebtedness bonds were issued in due time and put up for bids. The successful bidder was the El Paso National Bank in the person of W. H. Austin, who immediately resold them to an Eastern group and made a tidy sum thereby.[31] Mr. Morehead's feelings on learning of this successful *coup* can be imagined.

Austin and his bank were now enjoying the peak of their prosperity. In 1890 the El Paso National was doing more business than either of its rivals. Austin was a real power in the community. Besides achieving success in business he was a high-ranking Mason and a leader in the Elks' fraternity (he became Exalted Ruler in 1892).[32] It was almost a law of nature that he and Morehead should be at odds, and in 1890 they broke again. It is impossible to reconstruct just what happened after three-quarters of a century, but in June their differences were aired in the public prints. Austin published a column in the El Paso *Tribune* hinting that during his days as cashier of The State National Bank, he had noted financial irregularities. The implication was quite clear that Morehead was a subtle and successful crook.

Mr. Morehead reacted vigorously. In the columns of the *Times* for June 5 he answered Austin's charges, whatever they were (the files of the *Tribune* for this period have not been preserved):

> We had no transaction in scrip outside of the Bank and as an officer and stockholder he had as much to do with it as I did, all of which was legitimate. Mr. Austin was interested with me in all speculations and transactions outside of the Bank and shared in the profits with the exception of the El Paso Real Estate Co., during his stay in the Bank. If I have ever done anything illegitimate I don't know it, and if I have he is a party to it. He is free to betray any confidence that ever existed between us. I shall continue to act in my own interest together with my friends as I deem best and right and regret exceedingly to parade our private affairs before the people because I know they are disgusted with and deprecate in a great degree the exhibition of petty jealousies which seem to pervade every rank and calling. I fully realize that internal dissension must cease ere prosperity will come.

To emphasize his own peaceful disposition, Morehead called attention to the good relations which "we and our families sustained toward each other for several years here and for many years previous to our coming to El Paso," and drove the point home by quoting Austin's letter of January 25, 1881, thanking Morehead for his "many kindnesses" and assuring him of his hope the "I may some day be in condition to make you some return."

After that, nothing could repair the breach between the old master and the young one. Austin's men began to talk about the

"Morehead Gang" and to speak of themselves as the "Anti-Gang" group. During the campaign before the municipal election of 1891, they bolted the Democratic party, charging that the primaries were unfair. By this they undoubtedly meant that Morehead had his way and Austin did not in renominating Richard Caples for mayor. Two years later open warfare broke out between the two factions. Gang and Anti-gang were said to be at "sword's points," and there was heavy pressure on both leaders to run for the mayor's office. "The 'gang' would like to see C. R. Morehead made mayor," said the *Herald,* "but it will take a bitter fight and we do not believe Mr. Morehead will run. Mr. Austin is the strongest man in the 'anti-gang' and would draw most of the Republican votes."[33]

Mr. Morehead's image as a dark, sinister and subterranean worker was built up in every political utterance by his opposition. The editor of *El Centinela,* the Spanish-language newspaper, finally had enough of it. It would seem, he said "as though this modern Merlin would some dark night wave his magic wand and the burgh would be rolled up as a scroll and deposited in his breeches pocket. This El Paso Machiavelli . . . is guilty of the heinous crime of success and of being intelligent, farseeing and philosophic . . . but as we know him to be a good citizen, a liberal man in thought and deed with no fault other than his being 'a little smarter than the other fellows,' we would mildly suggest that they let him rest till he does something worthy of their attention."[34]

Morehead, as usual, wanted to make Pure Mesa Water the paramount issue in the coming election and banded together with twenty-seven other businessmen to put up $1,000 each to get the project going,[35] but the offer never came to anything, perhaps because something else was foremost in the minds of the citizens. Gambling was now the major question.

The reform element, in the field for the first time in 1889, was growing stronger and making more noise as the months went by. The Law and Order League, led by young lawyers Will and Richard Burges and their uncle Dr. William Yandell, plus assorted preachers, businessmen and housewives, were determined to put a stop to big-time gambling. They were not yet prepared to attack prostitution and the liquor business, but gambling they thought they could handle.

They had had a taste of success in 1890 when the Caples administration actually passed "An Ordinance to Restrain Gambling." Caples' idea of restraint, however, was simply to raise the price of sin. After January 1, 1890, a gambler had to pay $800 to stay open. The important operators were not bothered, of course, by such a tax, and could have stood one twice as big. Actually the tax worked in their interest by forcing the little gamblers out of business and leaving the pie to be cut by fewer people. The Wigwam saloon and gambling house cheerfully paid on January 13[36] and the rest followed suit with all convenient speed. The situation remained unchanged, big games running full blast every night with thousands of dollars on the tables and the gamblers banking money that should have gone for shoes and sausages. One wing of the Democrats – not Mr. Morehead's wing – became increasingly concerned about this community liability.

After Mr. Krakauer's shipwreck in 1889 the Republicans were disorganized and the Democrats were no longer obliged to hang together. In due time they made arrangements to hang separately. A group calling themselves Independent Democrats, the child of the Law and Order League, went into political action in the early months of 1893 and presented a slate of candidates for municipal office. Their choice for mayor was an honored and honorable lawyer named A. M. Loomis. The El Paso *Herald* was their organ and mouthpiece, and Editor J. A. (Uncle Jimmy) Smith began attacking "framed games" and infractions of state law by the owners of gambling saloons.[37]

The regular Democrats did as they were expected to do and nominated W. H. Austin as their candidate for mayor at the primaries in March, 1893, and this left Mr. Morehead, for the first time since 1881, with no place to go. He could hardly support Austin, though they saw eye to eye on the water question and the vice question, and the Independents didn't want him. When he declared for Loomis, people began to say that Loomis was Morehead's puppet. The Independents reacted violently and at once. "Morehead is willing, perforce" (Editor Smith declared), "to accept Loomis, but we happen to know that Loomis is not by any means or in any manner or sense a Morehead man."[38]

Mr. Morehead did not seem to mind very much. He kept right on supporting Loomis, welcome or not, and handled special situations as they arose according to his information and his conscience.

The water question was still throwing off sparks and creating an involved situation which was confused by the political campaign now in its final stages. The council was determined to do what it could to drill test wells in the valley as a start toward an independent water system. Mr. Morehead and his friends did not approve, and they were outraged when on January 23 a firm known as Rhodes Brothers were awarded a contract for sinking the wells. The word went round that the El Paso National Bank was backing the Rhodes Brothers, that they had made contact with W. H. Austin, that through his influence the contract had been railroaded through the council, and that he had profited personally thereby. Austin emphatically denied having received any "compensation" from Rhodes,[39] but the Morehead forces remained skeptical. Mr. Morehead signed a "Citizens' and Taxpayers' Call" demanding that all contracts be open to all bidders.[40] O. T. Bassett came out of his customary retirement to institute a suit in District Court against the city, and on February 1 Judge Buckler approved an injunction against the water bonds. The reason was that by law there must be enough money available from taxes to cover the obligations entered upon by the city. The wells could not be drilled without raising the tax rate above the legal limit.

As soon as this decision was recorded, the mayor vetoed the contracts with the well drillers on the very reasonable grounds that there would not be money enough to pay them.[41] It was a definite victory for the "Morehead gang," the first after a long series of reverses.

Austin was in trouble in other ways as well. A sufferer from Bright's disease, he was confined to his house when the news came that he had won the election and was now the mayor of El Paso. The jubilant "straights" came to rejoice with him at his home. Austin thanked them and promised that "with God's help he would carry out the platform,"[42] but he was in such bad condition that six days later he and his family were on a train headed for New York State and medical assistance. Through most of the summer and fall he was away in search of health, failed to find it, and on January 4, 1894, wrote a letter of resignation from Stafford Springs, New York. The council was not unduly surprised by the request and appointed Alderman Adolph Solomon acting mayor to serve until regular elections could be held in April.

The greatest blow of all came to Mr. Austin on August 2, 1893. The El Paso National Bank, a victim of bad loans and the panic of 1893, did not open its doors. Austin was in the city at the time and on August 1 told Lackland and Stewart, cashiers of the State and First National Banks, that they could get ready for a little extra business on the following day.[43] They knew what he meant and were prepared when nervous customers started withdrawing deposits. The flurry could have developed into a run, but it didn't. Instead, cash in greater quantities than ever began to flow into the State National and First National. As the *Times* reported it, the first new deposits came to the State National from Mr. A. Solomon, "amounting to about four thousand dollars. Then while the crowd was gathering about the corner Gov. Webster Flanagan came sauntering in with a leisurely smoke and a big roll of money, the latter of which he deposited and walked away with the same air of confidence that he would have exhibited had he placed his currency in the United States Treasury. Others, including A. M. Loomis, Z. T. White, Ketelsen and Degetau, R. F. Johnson, J. P. Dieter and Richard Caples hurried in to the State National, while such friends as Krakauer, Zork and Moye, T. J. Woodside, Kohlberg Bros., passed their money in to the receiving teller of the First."[44]

In spite of this display of confidence, the town was much shaken by the unexpected catastrophe, and for days and weeks people shook their heads and tried to understand how it could have happened as new rumors spread and new facts came to light.

Austin's explanation, when a reporter went to interview him, was that the closing was due to "continued stringency in the market and the shrinkage of deposits. We have ample resources to pay all our deposits four times over without touching the capital stock." He explained that President Bronson had gone to New York the preceding week to raise money on securities but could not make any headway.

This sounded good, but there was more uneasiness when the Bank of Juarez, a branch of the El Paso National, closed its doors too. The Las Vegas *Optic* was quoted as saying that "The president and cashier of the suspended El Paso National Bank owe that bank $67,952.35, while they owe the branch Bank of Juarez, $30,889.70."[45] Who provided these figures the article did not say, but since the Raynolds family were long-time Las Vegas residents, the chances are the information came from some knowledgeable person in the First National Bank of El Paso.

The next jolt to the tender sensibilities of the town came on August 20, 1893, when Austin left for treatment at McMinville, Tennessee. The pessimists at once deduced he had absconded and left the country. They were sure of it when on October 12 the United States Grand Jury indicted Bronson and Austin for misappropriation of the people's money.[46] On October 24, however, Austin was back in town and the *Tribune* pointed out with some triumph that he had not "skipped to Mexico."[47]

A year later, on October 26, 1894, the charges were dropped. U. S. District Attorney Culberson explained that he could not get needed evidence out of Mexico and he had no choice but to let the men go. There is no way of finding out what sort of evidence he had in mind.

When the story broke that Bronson and Austin were free, a wave of indignation swept the town. Depositors who had lost their shirts were understandably outraged. S. G. Etheridge of Clint, speaking (he claimed) "for the depositors," wrote to the *Times* on November 1. His heart was bleeding for the "impoverished and destitute depositors, clerks, mechanics, widows and children" who were "half crazed with the distress of destitution and loss of their little all." He lashed out at Bronson and Austin — "the two distinguished manipulators," for whom his kindest term was "boodlers."

In time people came to feel that Bronson was the major offender. It was true that Austin's uncles the Newman brothers were heavily involved in the affairs of the defunct bank and that their personal notes and the judgments against them were sold after the crash at a fraction of their face value[48]— facts which might have indicated that they were the villains. Nobody, however, had much to say against them. Austin likewise escaped severe criticism. After all, the country was in the grip of a panic. What had happened to him could have happened to anybody. He was probably guilty of nothing worse than bad judgment. Bronson, on the other hand, made some overt moves which finished him in the estimation of his fellow citizens. They came to the attention of Dr. Howard Thompson, Mr. Morehead's friend and personal physician, who commented as follows: "There is little doubt that Mr. Bronson in wicked spite, tried to bring on a financial panic. He is said to have gone down among the citizens of Utah Street [the red-light district] and spread the evil news that other banks in El Paso, particularly the State National, would have to close."[49]

Evidence of a sort that he did this appears in a cryptic paragraph in the *Times:*

> It is said that there is going to be the greatest explosion in financial circles some time in the future that El Paso ever knew. The El Paso National Bank failure will not be in it. A gentleman said last night that the eggs were laid some time ago, they were being hatched now, and the product would come later on. There is something foul in the atmosphere of the city without doubt.[50]

Having lit this fuse, Bronson went off to California where he became, among other things, a writer. A magazine article in 1910, in which he discussed "triggerfingeritis" in El Paso, solidified his unpopularity in his former home town. His description of El Paso in the early eighties as a lawless and blood-soaked battleground provoked indignant replies from a number of old timers and cost him any small shred of respect which may have lingered in people's minds.[51]

Unlike Bronson, W. H. Austin stayed with the ship and regained the good will and esteem of the community. With James L. Marr, his son-in-law, and some of the Newmans, he went into the real estate business. Austin Terrace, a first-class development in the eastern part of town, bears his name. For a while he worked for H. L. Newman in a private bank in Mr. Bronson's vacated quarters. His restless, adventurous nature involved him in a number of business enterprises in which he was mostly successful. He died of a heart attack in his home on San Antonio Street at the age of sixty-one on April 19, 1918.[52]

The State National Bank emerged from the depression of 1893 stronger than ever, and Mr. Morehead and his friends retained most of their influence in the affairs of the town. The reformers, however, never stopped putting on the pressure. In 1894 they gave El Paso its first taste of a real reform government, and El Paso did not like it.[53]

The mayor at this time was Robert F. Johnson, a wholesale liquor dealer appointed by the council when the regularly elected mayor refused to serve. Naturally he didn't like reformers at all, but they pushed him so hard that at last, in something like desperation, he declared that he would enforce the anti-gambling laws. He waited to make his proclamation, however, until he had a man on hand who was tough enough to do the enforcing. This was young Jeff Milton, known as a bandit tamer in Arizona and Texas, who gave up a job with the Pullman company to come to El Paso. He took the oath of office on August 10, 1894, and went immediately and effectively to work. He beat up the only gambler who dared to defy him and closed up the rest.[54]

At first the citizens, particularly the preachers and church members, were delighted, but after a few months even they realized that reform is bad for business. Bob Johnson, fed up, resigned before his term expired, and the next election was won by a poker-playing non-reformer named Robert Campbell.

Strangely enough, Morehead and Magoffin did not support him. His opponent was E. A. Shelton, the Law and Order League's candidate, a gentleman and a Christian who wanted to clean up the town and run the gamblers out once more. The Democrats were a house divided at this time and hardly anyone knew which way to vote. The State National Bank crowd for some reason chose to back Shelton, but their approval turned out to be a kiss of death. S. H. Newman, whose *Lone Star* had been defunct for eight years, resumed his role as municipal gadfly and told the regular Democrats to cross the party line and vote Republican. "Morehead and Magoffin," he warned them, "promise us nothing but reversion to mossback rule."[55]

Campbell won. His first act was to fire Jeff Milton. In a matter of hours the games were open again, and they stayed open.

In 1897 Joseph Magoffin went in as mayor. Mr. Morehead was prominently mentioned as a desirable candidate, but he could not be persuaded to run. Magoffin won by a very small margin – only twenty-nine votes – but he won, much to the disgust of the new editor of the *Herald*, a young Easterner named H. D. Slater.[56] With Slater's advent El Paso politics began to take on a new look. Slater was never in doubt of his own opinions and always sure that he was on the side of the angels. He was a good writer and a fierce opponent, all for the reformers and passionately averse to the old ways of doing things.

In the last days of Magoffin's incumbency Slater attacked "our miserable mayor" for failing to keep prostitutes off the streets. A group of reform-minded women had circulated a petition to keep the flesh-peddlers away from decent people, and Slater approved. On Sunday, however, "there were hack loads of them, gaudily dressed, parading the main streets."[57] Magoffin did nothing about this situation. Apparently he felt that the soiled doves had as much right as H. D. Slater to use the public thoroughfares.

The majority of the voters seemed to be on Magoffin's side, for they returned him to office in 1899 by a much larger majority than they had given him two years before. Slater fought him tooth and nail, even "exposing" Magoffin's record at the gambling tables (he had one).[58] But El Paso was not yet ready to judge its public officials on any such basis. Reform was coming, but not yet.

As the nineties drew to a close, El Paso was still growing fast and furiously and The State National Bank was still expanding. The old guard were still in charge, but the first break in their ranks came on January 4, 1898, when O. T. Bassett died in his bachelor quarters next door to his lumber yard. Since his wife's death of tuberculosis in 1882 he had led a somewhat retired life. He and his right-hand man Maury Edwards lived and worked in the same building, interested mostly in their business and making few outside contacts. His only son Charles, soon to be a major influence in the bank, was now attending Wabash College in Indiana after an abortive enrollment at Stanford.[59]

Mr. Bassett was aware that his time was short. His heart had been giving him trouble and he had told an Indiana friend some weeks before the end that "it would not be long." There was time for him to make some preparations. He made Charles promise that he would finish college before he took charge of the business and he arranged for C. R. Morehead to act as guardian. His affairs were in order when he went to bed, apparently in good spirits, on the evening of January 3. His friend and associate Joe Frist found him dead in bed the next morning.

"He did not mix with crowds," said the *Herald*, "but had a select coterie of friends for whom he could not do too much and all of them loved him for his good qualities and forgot his frailties."

"Politically," the story added, "he remained with the old element that ruled and governed El Paso in the early days."[60]

Mr. Bassett's untimely death (he was only forty-eight years old) removed an important pillar from the supporting structure of the bank, but new strength was at hand. A sign of the transition which the bank was about to undergo in the new century was the appearance on the roster of employees of the name of George D. Flory. A native of Maryland, he came to El Paso in the late eighties to work for the Wells Fargo Company. He left them when he became convinced that his services were worth more than his salary indicated. The story of The State National Bank for the next thirty years is largely the story of Charles N. Bassett and George D. Flory. At the close of the bank's second decade, they were standing in the wings, just ready to come on stage.

CHAPTER VI

UNDER NEW MANAGEMENT

• GEORGE FLORY was a special human being. No one who knew him ever forgot him. He stood among his fellow men like an oak among poplars and willows, though only a few could say they knew him well.[1]

He never talked much about his early days, even to his small circle of friends, and it is possible that he did not have much to remember. Born in 1868, he spent his boyhood on a farm near Hagerstown, Maryland. His family must have been poor, for he got no farther than the seventh grade in school. He treasured an old shotgun with which, he said, he used to hunt ducks on Chesapeake Bay – and that is all that can be said of his youth. When he came to El Paso in 1888, he left no close relatives behind. In later years he found some far-away cousins back in the old state, but at the age of twenty, when he arrived, he had nobody to claim kinship with but his uncle A. B. Roman, who for several years had been in charge of the local office of the Pacific Express Company. Roman had his living quarters and his business at 41 South El Paso Street, just below the Little Plaza, and there George Flory found his first home. He drove an express wagon for a living. In 1894 he became a clerk for Wells Fargo with an office at San Antonio and El Paso Streets at the other end of the block from The State National Bank.

Broad shouldered and powerfully muscled, Flory was an athlete and drifted naturally into association with like-minded young men. He became a member of the El Paso Volunteer Fire Department in the days when the firemen pulled their own hose carts – no mean feat on El Paso's sandy streets – and even pitted their skill and strength against the brawn and endurance of other hose companies from towns far away. One of the few pictures ever taken of George Flory shows him as a young man ready to take part in one of these contests. He was also an amateur boxer and played his share of baseball during the late eighties and early nineties when El Paso was baseball crazy and the El Paso Browns were considered the greatest team of all time. He belonged to the El Paso [Athletic] Club with rooms on South El Paso Street, where he met such other muscular men as Maury Edwards, manager of O. T. Bassett's lumber yard. They became friends, hunting and fishing companions, and eventually housemates. They were closer than brothers and they remained close for forty years.

Flory was straight American in most ways – intelligent, good at business, ruggedly honest, gruff in manner and quick tempered under stress, but capable of great loyalty and tenderness of heart. He had fine potential, but he might never have put his talents to their best use if Wells Fargo had really appreciated him. In 1896 he began to consider his situation and found that he was giving his company, at least in his own view, a good deal more than he was receiving. He went to the proper person and said so. The proper person told him the world was full of people in need of work, and if he didn't like his, he could walk off and leave it. He walked off and left it.

Either before or after this event, Mr. Lackland of the State National offered him a job. Since it has always been the policy of the bank to reject applications from people employed elsewhere, the offer probably came after his resignation. At any rate, Flory went to work at the bank as a bookkeeper and labored in the usual obscurity for some years. Like everybody else who has risen from the ranks at the State National, he learned the business by doing it – all of it – as bookkeeper, teller, stand-in for people out to lunch or out of town or in the hospital. He was good with figures, had a way with people, and possessed the kind of personal and financial judgment the bank needed. "He was always analyzing the situation," says Guyler Magruder, long-time vice-president; and as a matter of fact, he usually saw what was coming in financial and community matters long before it happened.

He was no Adonis, a fact which may explain his unwillingness to have his picture taken. He was of medium height and not particularly shapely or graceful, and his lips and eyebrows were thick and heavy. His habitual expression was somewhat dour and grim, and he looked like what he was – a tough *hombre.* But his gruffness was just a cover-up.

"He was the roughest person," Vice President Jack Moore will tell you, "and I believe he had the kindest heart I have ever known. I'd pass him every day. He'd stand right there by that swinging door we used to have to go through to get to the back of the building, and he wouldn't speak to you. You could speak to him, but he wouldn't speak back. So you didn't speak to him. You just went by him. One time I had a little problem and I asked somebody what to do. He said, 'You go talk to Mr. Flory.' I said, 'My God.' But I went to him and said, 'Mr. Flory, I need your help.' He said, 'Come on in here, Jack, and sit down.' So I asked my question and he told me exactly what to do. After that I still did not speak to Mr. Flory. He was a very unusual man."[2]

He was the soul of generosity, constantly giving things away, and served as a father substitute for the young men who worked under him. Always he was the best-loved man in the bank. And also he was the most feared. Any sort of double dealing or incompetence sent him into violent reaction. "If you never have been bawled out by Mr. Flory, you never have been bawled out," says Hal Daugherty (now Vice Chairman of the Board of Directors) – speaking from experience. If a daring young man suggested to Mr. Flory that he ought to have a raise, he was likely to get this sort of answer: "You get the hell out of here! When I want you to have a raise, I'll give it to you! Now get out or I'll take you down in the basement and whip you with a wet rope!"[3] It goes without saying that when Mr. Flory *did* get ready, the man got his raise.

All this was in the future, of course. Young Mr. Flory attended to business and gradually got ahead, thanks to his own talents and to the revolutionary changes that were beginning to take place in the bank.

One of these changes was the entry on the El Paso scene of Charles Nebeker Bassett, who took charge of his father's very considerable properties a few years after O. T. Bassett's death in 1898. He did not do so immediately since he had promised that he would finish college. Working as fast as he could, he graduated in about three years. Even so, he found time for some extra-curricular activities. As manager of the Wabash College baseball team, he is said to have achieved unusual success by hiring a few good players unconnected with the college. The relatives with whom he lived had kept him on short rations and made him account for every penny he spent. Then in 1898 his father died and suddenly he had all the money he wanted. He could afford to hire a whole team if he so desired. The chances are, of course, that the college authorities kept him from going very far in this direction.[4]

Naturally he enjoyed some social life. Will Hays, later famous as baseball commissioner and movie czar, was his friend and classmate (together they gave Wabash a chapel in later years) and he had other close friends with whom he kept in touch after college days were done. He was an earnest student, however, and spent an adequate amount of time on his books. He read Greek easily and was proud of it. His reading habits stayed with him throughout his life. When he had a home and a library, he often read until two or three in the morning, a large dictionary at his elbow. Naturally after one of these sessions he was apt to make a belated appearance at the bank. His habits as a banker, incidentally, were never regular.[5]

After he took his B.A. in 1901, he came at once to El Paso and prepared to enter the life of the town. Mrs. Joseph Magoffin had a "coming out" party to introduce him to the people who were to be his friends. It was a fitting gesture since Mr. Magoffin had taken Charley's father and mother in when they arrived in 1881 and had been a friend and business associate of the elder Bassett for many years.

Actually Charles had visited in El Paso more than once and knew his way around. He used to tell how when his father was paying attention to an El Paso woman, Charles would take out her younger sister on his bicycle-built-for-two. "I learned all the streets and avenues and alleys of El Paso that way," he would say with a laugh. Now he needed to make contact with something more substantial than the bicycle crowd.[6]

He owned some stock in the bank, of course, and became a director in 1902, but could not interest himself deeply in banking for some time after his arrival. There was the lumber business to learn, for one thing. Maury Edwards tried to teach him bookkeeping and it was a major effort. The balancing of debits and credits turned out to be a high hurdle, and Maury got exasperated when Charles kept asking why certain items were in particular places. "Because I say so, goddamit," he finally barked. "Put it there and you'll see why later on." Besides the commercial interests and real estate in El Paso, there was the lumber yard in Douglas, Arizona, the ranch in California, and the office buildings and real estate in Oklahoma City. For a young man whose business experience up to now had involved nothing beyond managing the Wabash College baseball team, these were heavy responsibilities, and it did not occur to Charley Bassett for some time that Mr. Morehead might need help in running his bank. The moment did come – eventually.

In the meantime he and George Flory formed a real Damon-and-Pythias type friendship which lasted without a cloud or shadow as long as they lived. With Maury Edwards they formed a bachelor triumvirate and set up housekeeping in a two-story dwelling on San Antonio Street across from the Baptist Church – the Toltec Club was later built on the site. Annie Scott Griggs, a loyal colored woman, looked after them. They welcomed Gene Fox and Brahan Cunningham into the fraternity and for some years led an existence which would seem to a good many men close to the ideal.

It was by no means a womanless existence. They knew every female in town worth knowing, and some not worth knowing – at least publicly. Stories still circulate about their escapades, and since they could afford to do what they wanted to do, some of their adventures took them far from the haunts of their Methodist and Baptist friends. They bought their whiskey by the gallon and lived according to their desires without apology or concealment.[7]

Mr. Flory made the point one time when a madam who kept a well-known house above Vic Salvini's place on the corner of Utah and Overland Streets was suing the bank for money she had lost on what she described as forged checks. Banks were liable for forged checks in those days. The chances are (George Matkin tells the tale) that the madam had signed the checks to pay her bills, leaving one of her girls to fill in the amounts, but she was trying to get the bank to make the checks good. Mr. Flory was on the witness stand and the prosecution was quizzing him:

"Mr. Flory, you know this lady?"
"Oh, yes, very well."
"You have visited her house?"
"Oh, yes, yes!"
"You go in by the back door, no doubt?"
"No, by God, I go in the front door and I have my money in my hand."[8]

They were always doing something unusual. Annie reported one time, with considerable amusement, that they had bought a whole turkey and made it all into turkey hash. This, of course, was a fine dish, but in Annie's experience it was made from left-overs. To make left-overs of a whole turkey was more than a little outlandish. She loved them all, however, and stayed with the Bassett family as long as she lived.

Neither George Flory nor Maury Edwards ever married, a fact which is hard to understand, for they were both very masculine men. Flory is said to have been "disappointed," and maybe he was. Nobody knows now. But there are many stories in circulation among people old enough to have known Flory about his being interested in this woman or that – contributing to the support of this woman or that – planning to marry this woman or that at the time of his death. The truth of the matter may be revealed by a story which Carl Hertzog tells.

At one time Carl developed a deep interest in riding, roping, and allied pursuits, and when the interest passed, he let it be known that his equipment was for sale. Guyler Magruder came to inquire about a saddle. Carl made him a price and said,

"A saddle is not much good without a horse. Why don't you buy the horse too?"

"No," replied Magruder, "I'll give you $250 for the saddle but I don't want the horse."

"Well, tell me what you have against horses."

"Mr. Flory taught me never to buy anything that eats."[9]

Bassett's heart remained more or less untouched until 1910. In November of the preceding year a young woman named Myra Powers came to town to be in the wedding party when Senator

Fall's daughter Carolyn married rancher Mahlon Everhart. Myra (from Illinois) and Carolyn (from El Paso and Three Rivers, New Mexico) were classmates at Mount Vernon Seminary for young ladies in Washington, D.C. The festivities ended tragically. On November 30, the night before the wedding, Margaret Bacon, a third classmate who had come to Texas with Myra, suffered a heart attack and died in the bathtub. The wedding plans were modified, of course. Myra, who was to have had a date with Charley Bassett that night, accompanied the body of the dead bridesmaid to her home in Indiana and did not meet Charley till a year later, when she returned to El Paso to visit the A. B. Falls and Carolyn Everhart. That started it. Charley telephoned Myra several times from Oklahoma City, when he was there on business. "Are you coming down to El Paso?," he would say. "I hope never again," she would reply. So he began traveling all the way up to Illinois to see her, and in 1915 they were married.[10]

The Flory-Bassett friendship was not a bit damaged by the new relationship. If anything, it was strengthened, for now Mr. Flory could adopt Charley Bassett's family in place of the one he never had. When the three Bassett girls came along, Flory loved them as if they were his own and left them with memories of a devotion which is rarely given by one human being to another.

All this took place on the circumference of Mr. Morehead's little universe. Morehead himself continued to be the dominant figure in the bank and in the community for some time after 1900. In fact, some of his finest hours were ahead of him at the turn of the century. He was not popular at all with an expanding segment of the community — the people who wanted to purify the town. For the others — those who liked the status quo or feared to change it — Mr. Morehead was still the man in whom they put their trust. There could be no question of his devotion to the welfare of the town. He just didn't believe that all this purity would work, and neither did most of his fellow citizens in the days of his glory.

The reformers never gave up in spite of defeat after defeat. Every time, they picked themselves up off the canvas and moved to attack again. In 1901 they thought they had won the fight at last when B. F. Hammett became mayor on a reform-oriented platform.

About all Mr. Hammett did for the cause, however, was to move the gamblers upstairs and order the saloon keepers to close their front doors on Sunday. He said nothing about the back doors. They remained open.

In 1903 the purifiers determined to make a supreme effort. For mayor they nominated their best man – Sheriff James H. White. It would have been hard to find a better or more popular citizen in El Paso than Jim White. He seemed unbeatable, and the Straight Democrats realized that only their best would be good enough. In every election since 1889 Morehead's name had been mentioned as the right man for the job, and he was urged earnestly to offer himself as a candidate. Every time he had sidestepped the responsibility. Now he could not. When the primaries were over, it was Morehead against White.

Feeling ran high during the campaign. All the best people appeared to be for White and it seemed impossible that he could lose. Even the children were shouting for him. On the playground at Sunset School they were chanting a rhyme:

> White, White, he's all right!
> Morehead, Morehead, he's a sorehead!

How far Morehead had sunk in the estimation of the reform element was evident in H. D. Slater's editorial commenting on the candidates. In the *Herald* for April 8, 1903, he remarked that the two rivals had been residents of El Paso about the same length of time, "yet what a contrast!"

> Morehead's political record for two decades is one long list of wrongs perpetrated against the community, through lending his influence and aid to the corrupt elements in their constant warfare against decency and law. His is a record of wrong political methods and unfortunate political associations. His political record cannot stand the light. It is light he hates, hence his retiring pose, his unwillingness to have his name connected with the evil machinations in which he takes a leading part.
>
> His domination is a constant menace to the community.

It must have been hard indeed on Mr. Morehead to read such a bitter denunciation, but he was to hear worse before the campaign was over. As before, he wanted to talk about municipal ownership of the water supply (El Paso was still fighting that battle), but the opposition insisted on discussing gambling, saloons, and prostitution – always making Morehead out to be the supporter and defender of all the vice and villainy on the border. It made him sick, but he never openly said so. He sat by while Waters Davis, the Burges brothers, H. D. Slater, James A. Dick, and several hundred of their friends made him their whipping boy at rallies and assemblies. The night before election the reformers all gathered in the plaza to listen to speeches and cheer their candidates. They were confident of victory and went home jubilant.[11] But next day the machine functioned as it always had. Both sides voted everybody who could be persuaded or paid to go to the polls. Mexico cooperated as usual by sending her sons in "hordes" to vote in the American election, and more of them voted for Morehead than for White. Once more the Reformers tasted defeat.

You would never have known it from the way they went to work on Morehead. In a matter of weeks, they had organized a Citizens' Reform League with Waters Davis at the head and Richard Burges backing him up. They started a tremendous campaign to educate the public concerning the prevalence of gambling and its influence on the community. They declared that no less than 600 professional wheelers and dealers were in residence in forty licensed gambling halls, and they went on from there. The pressure increased day after day and week after week. It was so severe that every public official felt the strain.

There was even high tension in the city council. Alderman Charman grumbled publicly that Morehead "wanted to run everything," and Alderman John Burton actually came to blows with his chief in front of City Hall when a new water company was organized without the mayor's blessing. Mr. Morehead retired to his office, where a doctor attended to his bruised eye. Reporters were not admitted.[12]

In September of 1904, after a little more than a year in office, he began to show signs of giving way. Word went round that the gambling houses were going to close. He issued a public denial, but Alderman Harry Charman, interviewed in his citadel (a cigar store) revealed that the houses and gambling saloons on Utah Street had been ordered to close. The rest of the city would remain open, but no new licenses would be issued to gamblers, and the gambling industry would gradually die out. Charman did not like what he reported and grumbled that El Paso would never be a Sunday School.[13]

Utah Street remained open for business, showing no signs of stress, but on October 5 Chief of Police Wooten resigned. Florence J. Hall, the new chief, said he thought the mayor meant to limit gambling. The mayor, of course, said nothing at all.

On October 19 the Citizens' League assembled and placed a thousand signatures on a petition calling for an end to open gambling. On November 10 another rally was held, attended by so many people that they could not all get into the Airdome, the open-air pavilion across from City Hall. They all cheered for the end of gambling in El Paso and added more names to the petition.

Early next day a committee called on the mayor and asked him to give them a direct answer to one question: Was it true or was it not true that he was going to close up the gamblers or put them out of sight? Everyone had heard that such was his intention.

Mr. Morehead was more than a little exasperated. "I have made no such statement," he told them. "There are more liars in El Paso than any place I ever saw."[14]

The Citizens' Reform League now had 1,500 names on its petition. The leaders presented it to Sheriff J. H. Boone and asked him to enforce the law. Boone shuffled and shadow-boxed for a short time and then, to everyone's astonishment, he declared that he was paid to enforce the law, he believed in enforcing the law, and he would begin at once to enforce not just the gambling law but every other law as well.

In short, Morehead had ostensibly given in. Neither he nor any of his friends and supporters believed he ought to do so. Their real feelings were betrayed at the next meeting of the city council. The aldermen discussed ways and means of making up for the $65,000 deficit in city funds which would be the result of cutting off fines paid by prostitutes and license fees paid by gamblers. They quite obviously thought that the city was going to feel a financial pinch.[15]

What Mr. Morehead was thinking we have no means of knowing, but there is a pattern in his actions from this moment on which makes it seem more than probable that he intended to give the reformers an overdose of their own medicine. In mid-November he closed the gambling houses and shortly thereafter ordered the cribs and dance halls to close. Saturday, November 19, 1904, was supposed to be the end of everything, and a large crowd of drunk and tearful devotees made the rounds of all the houses and saloons to say farewell. It was onc of El Paso's most memorable nights. The following day the girls departed for less virtuous communities. The gamblers had already crossed to Juarez.

The next move was Sheriff Boone's. He announced in the columns of the newspapers that all the laws were going to be enforced, and he advised the citizens to read the statutes. According to the Texas "blue laws" no business could be open on Sunday. A man could not even buy a cigar. There would be no amusements of any kind – no concerts at the Myar Opera House, no plays or variety shows at theatres. Since all businessmen, even shoeshine boys, were forbidden to operate, the brewery and the A. S. and R. smelter would have to close down, though in these enterprises the fires had to be kept going regardless of blue laws. It cost $1100 to shut down the smelter for one day. Boone actually arrested the smelter employees when he caught them working on Sunday. He even issued orders to bring in a group of citizens who had participated in a turkey shoot – on Tuesday. He said they had violated the anti-gambling laws.[16]

All over the country El Paso became a laughing stock. Papers throughout the West noted with amusement that the community was down with an attack of morals and predicted that the sickness would soon pass. To make matters worse, Juarez profited tremendously by the shut-down. All the drinkers and gamblers simply crossed the bridge and functioned as before. Several thousand of them visited Mexico on the Sunday after the closing.[17]

It did not take El Paso long to get the message. The first sign of a change of heart appeared when six well-known businessmen asked to have their names taken off the petition which had started Sheriff Boone on his near-fatal course. Their request was published in the *Times*.[18]

Three weeks after the closing, the town had had enough. The

Legal Tender Saloon stayed open on Sunday, December 3, and Max Miller, the proprietor, was arrested as he had expected to be. The next day in justice court a jury refused to convict him. In a matter of hours the gamblers had come back from across the river, and all was as before. Mr. Morehead had made his point.

In doing so, however, he had prepared his own political funeral. By this time C. E. Kelly, a politician of great shrewdness and resourcefulness, had built up an effective political machine. In many ways he was Morehead's kind of man. He too liked to exercise influence from the background and did his ordering and arranging in a little office behind Kelly and Pollard's drug emporium. He too thought that vice was here to stay and should be taxed rather than eliminated. He too was all for municipal ownership of city water services. A practical politician like Morehead, he used the tools that were ready to his hand for what he considered the welfare of his community. In 1902 he became city treasurer and held the office until 1910, when he became mayor in name as well as in fact.[19]

He broke with Morehead because he thought Morehead was wrong in going along with the reformers, even for those educational three weeks. He believed that Morehead and Magoffin and the old "gang" were due for a long stay in the pasture.[20] As he moved toward control of the city government, the strong-arm boys on both sides began to bristle and there was one big fight in the Coney Island Saloon when blows were struck and shots were fired,[21] but there was no trouble after that. J. U. Sweeney, Kelly's candidate, went in as mayor in 1907, and Kelly himself became the city's chief executive in 1910. In that year El Paso finally took charge of its water supply and Mr. Morehead's long battle was won, though he was no longer at the head of the troops.

By now he was passing through the final years of his active life and a new generation was growing up around him in the bank. In 1908 J. C. Lackland, cashier since 1886, was removed by death.[22] George D. Flory was promoted from the post of assistant cashier, which he had occupied for only a year, to replace him. Charles N. Bassett bought Lackland's stock, thereby increasing his own influence in the bank, though he was not yet ready to step into a leading role. An energetic and public-spirited man, he was carrying a full load already. When the United States moved into the First World War, he began a long series of involvements with civic and national affairs. Among other responsibilities, he was food administrator for the town and regional director of Liberty Bond sales. He had plenty to do without trying to run The State National Bank.

For two years the Great War was the major concern of everybody in El Paso, women and men alike. The bank and its staff were involved in many ways — scrap drives, fund raising, bond sales, rationing. The flower of El Paso's young manhood went off to fight in France — some of them to die there. One of the heroes who came back alive was Paul H. Anderson, an employee of The State National Bank, who had the unique distinction of receiving both the Distinguished Service Cross and the French Croix de Guerre in a ceremony held in San Jacinto Plaza. Serving as a private in the 160th Infantry, Paul had acted as a courier maintaining liaison between the companies of his battalion on the firing line. On November 1, 1918, he was severely wounded but continued trying to keep communications open. His citation read: "Private Anderson went on two missions for his battalion commander, which necessitated passing through heavy machine gun and shell fire, not mentioning the fact he had been wounded."

He was shipped home before the decorations could be awarded, but word came to General Erwin at Fort Bliss, and he arranged the presentation ceremony on the evening of May 15, 1919, as the climactic moment of a great "Welcome Home" celebration in San Jacinto Plaza for 650 returning servicemen.

Years later, during World War II, a major in the Dental Corps, irritated because of some difficulty in the bank's handling of his wife's account, wrote a nasty letter to Paul Anderson complaining of the inefficiency and irresponsibility of the 4F's on the State National staff. A bank official replied to this blast, informing the major of Paul's record as a soldier. A subdued and embarrassed officer came all the way from San Antonio to El Paso to apologize in person.

Paul Anderson stayed with the bank, one of its most beloved and useful executives, until his death of a heart attack on July 21, 1949.

During the war years it was impossible to make major changes in the bank's organization, but after the armistice the time was ripe for reorganization and expansion. Capable young men had been joining the staff for some time. L. J. Gilchrist signed on in 1905; Walter W. Scott (later head of the Trust Department) in 1913; George Matkin (today chairman of the board) in 1917; R. W. McAfee in 1917 (from Bassett Lumber Company); Guyler Magruder in 1919; Forrest M. Smith in 1920.[23] These were all extremely competent businessmen who rose to high positions in the State National or in other banks. They were large-calibre people in a small-calibre operation, and Bassett and Flory knew it, but their hands were tied. Mr. Morehead did not want to go after business aggressively. He was content with what came naturally as the town grew – like the new accounts that came with the arrival of the militia from the East during World War I, when El Paso was introduced to the one-dollar bill. The Mexicans and the old settlers liked the clink of silver but the soldiers were not used to carrying all that weight around. Likewise during the Mexican Revolution, between 1910 and 1920, some new money came to town with *Porfirista* refugees. But beyond question the bank could have had a great deal more business just by asking for it.

Mr. Morehead would not ask. The bank suited him just fine the way it was. He wanted the management to be in his hands, and he saw no reason why he should accept dictation from anybody on these matters. He had founded the bank. He had made the bank. He had kept the bank going. It was his bank.

George Matkin saw what was happening when he joined the staff in the spring of 1917. George was a senior in high school, where he had not been very happy or very sure of the value of what he was doing. He liked to study when he was learning something that applied to his special interests, but books for books' sake were not for him. He had been delivering papers for years, had been offered a job at the *Herald*, and had every intention of accepting when a telephone call came to the principal's office. It asked that a boy from the graduating class be sent down to the bank for a job interview. Since George was the only boy in the senior class, he was automatically recommended, and he went down for a session with Mr. Flory.

Flory behaved in characteristic fashion. In the course of their conversation, George asked about salary. "Your future is more important than what you are going to make," Flory said.

"Well, I've been offered a job at the newspaper and I just wanted to know how the offers would compare."

"How much did they offer you?"

"Sixty dollars a month."

"You come on down here and work for us."

George thought he could expect sixty-five or better, but sixty was what he got.

His instruction were to show up at eight next day, and at five minutes before eight, George was at the door. It was locked. He shook it and knocked gently. Mr. Morehead appeared in the doorway and asked George what he wanted.

"Mr. Flory told me to report here at eight."

"Come inside and sit down. Somebody will be here after a while and tell you what to do."

So the boy sat down opposite Mr. Morehead, who was opening the mail. There weren't many letters, but he made a little ceremony of dealing with each one. His procedure was to take a pair of scissors out of a drawer and cut off the end of each envelope. Then he would put the scissors down, take out the contents, throw the envelope in wastebasket, hold the letter up close to his eyes, and read it. He would repeat the performance with the next item. Finally he picked up a communication from a bank at Marfa. George could see the heading through the paper. He noted that a check was included. Mr. Morehead, following his routine, tossed everything but the letter into the wastebasket. The check went in too. George saw it, and was faced with a terrific problem. Was it his business on his first day at work to point out that the boss had made a serious error? Finally he decided that he had better say something.

"Mr. Morehead, I think you threw a check into that waste basket."

"Oh, did I?"

He picked up the the wastebasket, dumped the contents on the table, and began to hunt for the check.[24]

It was obvious to everybody that he was not the Morehead of old. His health was failing; there were signs of approaching senility; he could not stand even minor changes in his business and way of life. Every morning without fail he was at his desk at seven going through his mail, carefully gathering up all pins and paper clips and putting them in boxes.[25]

The paper clips were a sign of what was wrong. The bank was in a rut, and as long as Mr. Morehead had his way, it was not going anywhere. The only officer on the staff, besides Mr. Flory, who had any get-up-and-go was L. J. Gilchrist, an assistant cashier who was everybody's friend and something of a man-about-town. The other banks had more money and more business, and there was considerable doubt among businessmen that the State National had any future at all. Ike Wolf took George Matkin aside one time when they met on the street and told him he was wasting his time there. If Mr. Gilchrist left, the whole thing would fold up. Ed Holschneider, who moved to Mexico City when Germans became objects of suspicion during World War I, told him the same thing. "The bank will never amount to anything, and neither will you if you stay here," he warned George.

As a matter of fact, Gilchrist did leave, to become vice-president of the American Trust and Savings bank. It didn't seem to make much difference. Only two depositors withdrew their accounts and followed Gilchrist to his new home, and one of them went broke shortly after. George came to the conclusion that the institution was what counted, and he still thinks so.

Matkin was not yet in a position to do much about the situation, but Charley Bassett and George Flory were. They knew that Mr. Morehead would have to be laid on the shelf, and gradually they determined to do what had to be done. It worried them terribly. Bassett used to walk the floor at night wondering how he could either persuade Mr. Morehead to get off his swivel chair, or move him off.[26] He finally came to the conclusion that the matter must be handled firmly and effectively. The worst mistake would be a half-hearted effort. He had tried repeatedly to get Mr. Morehead to think about enlarging or rebuilding or moving the bank. That would be a first step. Mr. Morehead would not listen. Bassett suggested increasing the bank's capitalization, which stood at only $110,000 after being doubled in 1914. This too Mr. Morehead vetoed. Insurrection was the only course left.

Bassett felt that the proxies of the St. Louis stockholders were the key to the situation. Mr. Morehead held them, and voted them as he wished. Those 300-odd shares might make the difference. Mr. Bassett left town for a few days (he was often away on business and nobody suspected what he had in mind) and turned up in St. Louis. He went to the stockholders and explained the situation to them. Would they authorize him to vote their stock at the stockholders' meeting? They would and did, and Bassett got ready for the next annual meeting, which was scheduled for January 4, 1921.

Mr. Morehead's personal difficulties by now had become almost insurmountable. Guyler Magruder came down at seven o'clock one morning late in 1919. The books had to be posted and it was his job to keep them up to date, so he arrived early. Mr. Morehead was there too, opening his mail.

"I heard a big crash back there," Guyler remembers. "I went back to see about it and he'd got up on his chair to lower a window shade and fallen. He was lying on the floor. I picked him up and put him back in the chair. His left arm was limp. He said, 'Where's my arm?' I said, 'Here's your arm.' I lifted it and it was broken in several places. It never healed."

With the man in such shape as this, it seemed more cruel and brutal than ever to displace him, but on the other hand it seemed more necessary than ever.

Mr. Morehead knew what they were going to do. Word about the proxies got back to him, and Bassett and Flory decided that they had better move at once. Instead of waiting for the annual meeting, they fired their first shot at the monthly meeting of the Board of Directors held on March 20, 1920. Just before this assembly Flory said to Matkin, "He's *got* to do it. We're going to *make* him do it!"

The battle opened with a motion to call a stockholders' meeting for April 20. The Directors' Minutes, in R. W. McAfee's careful hand, tell what followed.

> The question was called for and C. R. Morehead, presiding officer, declined to put said question; whereupon he was requested to put the question and declined so to do; thereupon the question was put by the vice president, C. N. Bassett, and a vote was taken, the result of which was as follows: C. N. Bassett, Geo. D. Flory and R. W. McAfee voted "yes," meaning thereby they voted in favor of the motion to call a meeting of the stockholders; Joseph Magoffin declined to vote and C. R. Morehead voted in the negative, that is to say, against calling a meeting of stockholders.
>
> It was and is accordingly ordered that the proper officer cause to be issued and published a call for a shareholders meeting to be held on the 20th day of April, 1920 . . . said meeting of the shareholders to be for the purpose of increasing the capital stock of the bank, and all other such business relating to the bank and its welfare as may come before the meeting.

George Matkin says that Mr. Morehead brought with him to this meeting an old lawyer friend of his named Stanton, hoping with his help to stand off the assault.[27] He was outmaneuvered, however, and he left the bank that day to return only once more in his lifetime.

Magruder was down early one morning not long after the overthrow and saw Mr. Morehead come in and go to his office. He got a box and put in it all his personal effects, wiping out forty years of his business life. He did it all with one hand, his left arm still being useless, and he walked out as he had come in, still his own man asking no odds of anybody. He had not looked around, and he had not spoken a word. The door closed behind him for the last time.

He was not present at the stockholders' meeting on April 20. Bassett presided and Maury Edwards voted the St. Louis proxies. George Flory moved to increase the capital stock of the bank by declaring a stock dividend of 100%, increasing the capitalization to $220,000. Next he moved that the bank sell 800 shares at $250 a share. Of the $200,000 thus realized, $80,00 would be added to the capital stock, which would then stand at $300,000. Finally he presented a resolution to extend the corporate existence of the organization for twenty years from March 8, 1921. All motions were passed unanimously. It was the beginning of a new day for the State National.

At the next regular meeting of shareholders, held on January 11, 1921, the new management consolidated its gains. Bassett with 656 shares (after the stock division) and Flory with 600 were the largest sharcholders. The St. Louis shares added up to 611 – 2051 shares represented in all.

The new directors (the April meeting had approved a number between five and twenty-five) were C. N. Bassett, H. L. Birney, Juan F. Brittingham, B. F. Darbyshire, George D. Flory, Maury Kemp, Charles R. Morehead, R. W. McAfee, Charles M. Nebeker and Ed Sanders.

At the director's meeting which followed the general assembly of stockholders, a new office was created. Maury Kemp moved and George Flory seconded a proposal to make C. R. Morehead Chairman of the Board of Directors. "He being absent, C. N. Bassett presided at the meeting of said Board of Directors and announced that the Board would proceed to elect officers for the said bank for the year 1921."

C. N. Bassett, quite naturally, was made president. Flory was vice president. R. W. McAfee was cashier. Charles M. Nebeker, John P. Ronan, and Walter W. Scott were assistant cashiers. And so the newly launched ship, with a new complement of officers, spread her sails and began to steer a course through the high seas of the 1920's.

Mr. Morehead did not last long after he lost his bank. He stayed at home, surviving three bouts with pneumonia, until his death on December 15, 1921, at the age of eighty-six. During his final months his friends came to see him, pay their respects, and talk of old times. After the funeral his old acquaintance J. D. Ponder, who had known him since 1889, paid tribute to this truly remarkable man. He spoke of his moral and physical courage, his social graces, his devotion to his town, his unobtrusive charities. "I know of a half dozen newsboys who went to the back door of his bank every Saturday," Ponder wrote, "to get the money Mr. Morehead was sending their mothers to enable the humble family to have enough to eat the following week. He loved all boys and always carried a handful of dimes for them."

Ponder commented on the bitter campaign of 1889 when Morehead was defeated in the mayor's race. "The estrangement of friends through the contest hurt him keenly, but he was too proud and sensitive to make advances for reconciliation."

That was the key to the man's character. Proud, sensitive and shy, he protected himself as best as he could by staying in the background, but duty pushed him into the midst of the strife sometimes, and he suffered for it. He could have died a bitter man, but he did not. "A year ago," Ponder said, "Mr. Morehead told me he did not harbor an ill thought against any person living and that he wanted the good will of all men."[28] This may have been Charles R. Morehead's way of sending a little message to Charles Bassett and George Flory, from beyond the grave, to tell them that he understood what they had done and forgave them.

Chapter VII

CRISIS

• What valley forge was to George Washington, the events of 1931 were to The State National Bank. It was a time of testing from which the organization emerged triumphant, but it was hard going for a while.

Through the wild and unstable twenties Bassett and Flory kept the ship on course and going steadily forward. The moment the management was securely in their hands, they began to carry out their plans for expansion and improvement. On October 1, 1920, they made application to the Federal Reserve Board for a permit to act as "trustee, executor, administrator, registrar of stocks and bonds, guardian of estates, assignee, receiver, committee of estates of lunatics;"[1] in short, for a Trust responsibility. This was the beginning of a department which now manages assets worth $87,000,000 and over 100,000 acres of land.[2]

Walter Scott, who had been an employee since 1913 and was due for promotion, asked Mr. Flory who was going to run the new department. "I am," Mr. Flory growled, "and you are going to do the work."[3] That was exactly how it was arranged, too, until Flory decided that Scott was ready to take charge. In 1923 he became Trust Officer (with R. W. McAfee), and headed the Trust Department until 1970.

Another Flory-Bassett dream which could now come true was the construction of a new bank building. The one they were occupying, built in 1882, had long been outgrown and outmoded. In October, Trost and Trost went to work drawing up plans for a bigger and better structure. J. E. Morgan was the contractor; Remington and Company of Los Angeles designed the interior; marble was furnished by the Vermont Marble Company of Dallas; and Warner and Woodruff of Los Angeles installed the concealed lighting fixtures.[4] Construction began in March, 1921, and was completed in less than a year. Bassett and Flory were in a hurry.

Since the new bank was to occupy the old site, the business had to be moved temporarily, and early in 1921 the entire operation was shifted to rented quarters in the Blumenthal Building on the corner of South El Paso and San Francisco Streets. The City National Bank had just vacated the premises and gone to a sumptuous new location in the Two Republics Building, later the home of the El Paso National Bank. The Blumenthal Building offered more spacious accommodations than the old State National[5] but Mr. Bassett was anxious to get into the new building. It was just a bit embarrassing to be operating in a facility that had been considered inadequate by a competing bank.

At his urging the contractors finished the new State National building well ahead of schedule. By the middle of January, 1922, the return from exile had begun. Completion of the moving process was announced in a full-page advertisement in the *Herald* of January 28 inviting the public to come in for a visit between eight a.m. and six p.m. the following Monday.

The public was deeply impressed. The new building was 122 by 48 feet — had twice as much floor space as the old one. The exterior was designed in classic Roman style with arched grilled windows and heavy bronze doors. Above a four-foot-high granite base, white terra cotta walls gleamed in the sun. Inside, steel girders supported the roof, eliminating pillars and making the interior one great, lofty room. The floors and tellers' cages were of San Saba marble, and a marble stairway led to the basement. There was a mezzanine floor which housed the law firm of Kemp and Nagle, attorneys for the bank, and a hydraulic service elevator connected basement and lobby. Everything was shining, expensive, and up-to-date — 4,000 safety-deposit boxes, oil-burning heating plant, "hold-up" buttons in case of an attempt at robbery, nine tellers' cages, space for six officers, and ample quarters in the rear for the bookkeepers and record keepers. The cost was $250,000 and the officers felt that it was money well spent.[6]

The bank went after business, and income rose steadily. Dividends, set at four percent in 1919, returned to six percent in 1920 and never again fell below that figure. Profits amounted to

First location of The State National Bank of El Paso on the northeast corner of East San Antonio and El Paso streets. Picture was taken on Jan. 1, 1882.

[EL PASO PUBLIC LIBRARY]

'Downtown' El Paso in 1882, looking north from the intersection of East Overland and El Paso streets. The State National Bank can be seen at left center.

[WYNDHAM K. WHITE]

[PHOTOGRAPHS SUPPLIED THROUGH COURTESY OF NAMES IN BRACKETS]

West side of El Paso street in 1881, as seen above the 'parapeto' on roof of the Butterfield Stage building. At left is the Davis Block, on the corner of West Overland street. Central Hotel, right center, was on Little Plaza, where the White House Department Store is now located. [EL PASO PUBLIC LIBRARY]

East San Antonio street in 1886, as seen from roof of the Wm. A. Irvin building. The State National Bank's new home, on the corner of S. Oregon, is at right center. Across the street, construction is underway on the Bronson Block, where the original El Paso National Bank opened on Jan. 1, 1887. [JOHN G. OECHSNER]

An early view of The State National at its second location, on the southwest corner of East San Antonio and Oregon streets. El Paso's premier bank conducted business in this building for four decades. [EL PASO PUBLIC LIBRARY]

The bank's 'vault' – a small gold safe now in the SNB archives.

Some original Safe Deposit Boxes – the ultimate in security during early years.

CHAS. R. MOREHEAD
President
[MRS. DEXTER MAPLE, SR.]

OSCAR T. BASSETT
Director
[MRS. C. N. BASSETT]

HENRY L. NEWMAN
Director
[S. H. NEWMAN III]

W. H. AUSTIN
Cashier
[EL PASO TIMES]

The State National started with three officers, Charles R. Morehead, President; Joseph Magoffin, Vice President; William H. Austin, Cashier, and two directors, Oscar T. Bassett and Henry L. Newman.

Staff of The State National in 1886. From left, standing: J. C. Lackland, cashier; L. M. Turner, bookkeeper; Tom Grigsby, janitor; Seated: Wyndham Kemp, attorney; Charles R. Morehead, president; Joseph Magoffin, vice president; Hep Russell, assistant cashier.

[SNB ARCHIVES]

Refugees from the flooding Rio Grande, circa 1885 – on site of the present El Paso Public Library.

[WYNDHAM K. WHITE]

Campbell street side and rear of El Paso's Central School, which faced on Myrtle street, as seen from roof of the Pierson Hotel in 1885. Solomon Schutz, wealthy merchant, lived in the two-story house at right center, on northwest corner of Myrtle and Campbell. [C. L. SONNICHSEN]

Southern Pacific Depot on Main street, near Kansas, in 1882. Mountains in the background are in Mexico, and the barren area at right center was the Public Square, later to become San Jacinto Plaza. [LEON C. METZ]

Circus parade coming west on St. Louis street (now Mills) and turning into Little Plaza (now Pioneer Plaza) circa 1885. [W. H. MITCHELL]

The present Sunset Heights area, upper left, as seen from the Pierson Hotel in the mid-1880s, with the S.P. Depot in the foreground. The buildings at top center were in "Mesa Gardens," a popular recreation park near what is now W. Yandell Drive, W. Rio Grande and N. Santa Fe streets. [U.T. EL PASO ARCHIVES]

First bridge over the Rio Grande — built by the Southern Pacific Railroad in 1881, north of El Paso near the present Cement Plant. This bridge was replaced by the one in use today, some yards to the south. The tracks paralleling the river were those of the A.T. & S.F. [PONSFORD BROTHERS]

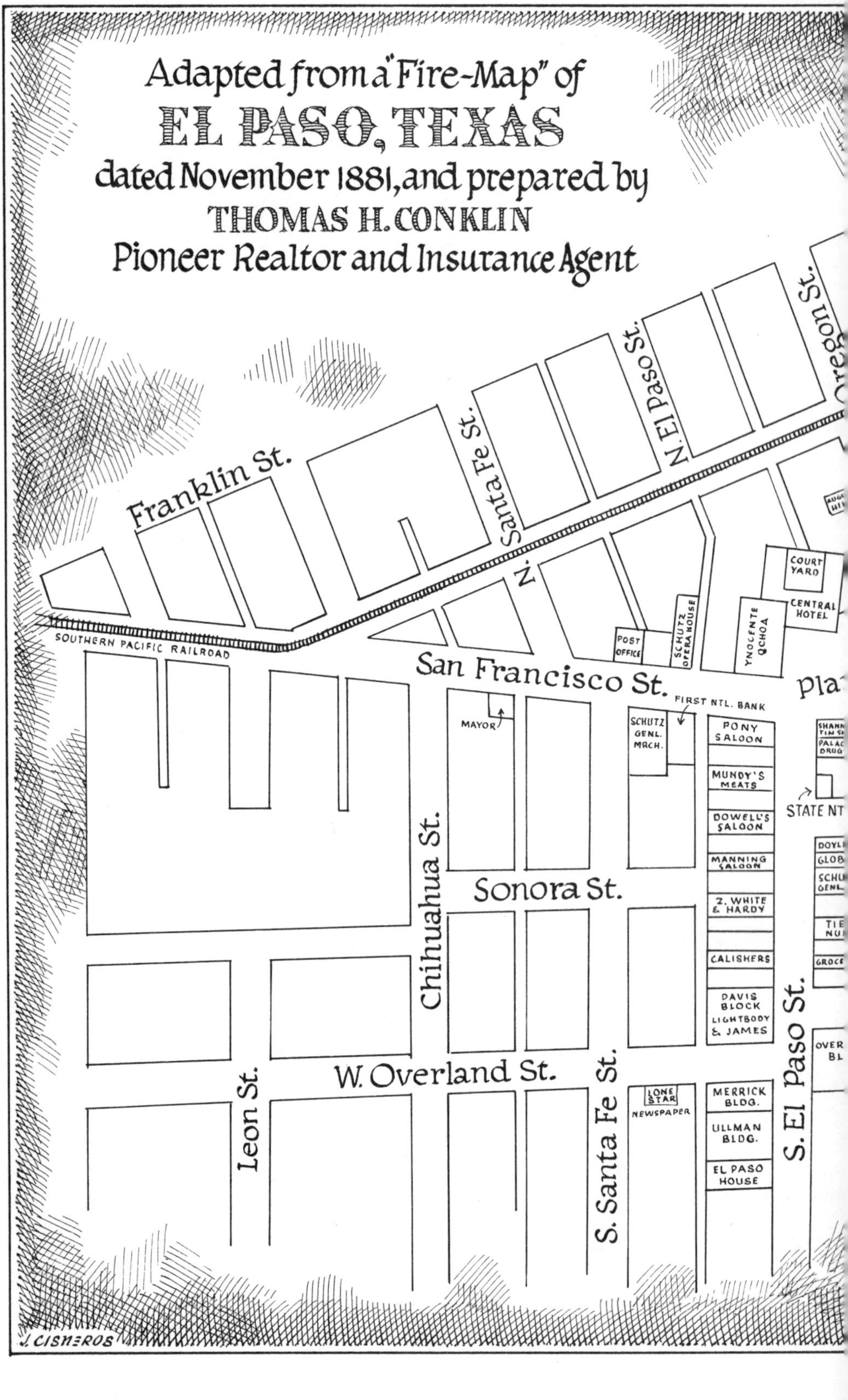
Adapted from a "Fire-Map" of
EL PASO, TEXAS
dated November 1881, and prepared by
THOMAS H. CONKLIN
Pioneer Realtor and Insurance Agent
Franklin St.
N. Santa Fe St.
N. El Paso St.
Oregon St.
SOUTHERN PACIFIC RAILROAD
COURT YARD
CENTRAL HOTEL
POST OFFICE
SCHUTZ OPERA HOUSE
YNOCENTE OCHOA
San Francisco St.
FIRST NTL. BANK
MAYOR
SCHUTZ GENL. MRCH.
PONY SALOON
MUNDY'S MEATS
DOWELL'S SALOON
MANNING SALOON
Z. WHITE & HARDY
CALISHERS
DAVIS BLOCK
LIGHTBODY & JAMES
STATE NT
Chihuahua St.
Sonora St.
W. Overland St.
Leon St.
S. Santa Fe St.
S. El Paso St.
LONE STAR NEWSPAPER
MERRICK BLDG.
ULLMAN BLDG.
EL PASO HOUSE
J. CISNEROS

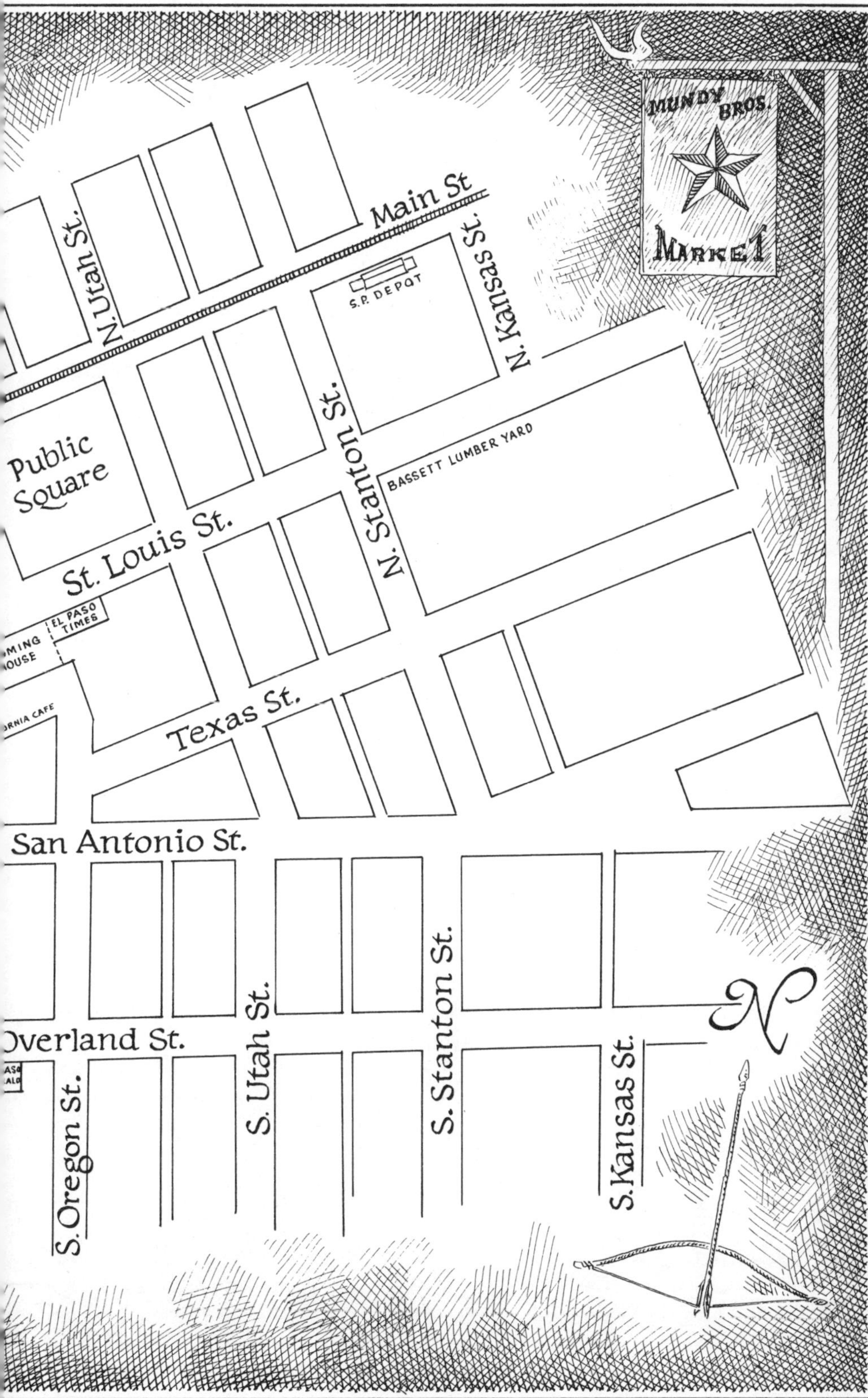

[JOSE B. CISNEROS *for El Paso County Historical Society*]

Fort Bliss officers quarters, when the Post was at Hart's Mill – on the Rio Grande – in 1881. Authorization for The State National Bank to "commence business" was received via Army Signal Corps wire. [LEON C. METZ]

The new Fort Bliss in 1895 – on La Noria mesa east of El Paso. All buildings seen in this picture are still in use. [ANGELA B. COONS]

El Paso's mule-drawn streetcar has just turned west onto St. Louis street (now Mills) in 1884. On the right is the office of the O.T. Bassett Lumber Company, now the site of the 22-story State National Building. [U.T. EL PASO ARCHIVES]

Second location of Bassett Lumber Company, on the southeast corner of Overland and Virginia streets. [U.T. EL PASO ARCHIVES]

Interior of The State National Bank in 1909 as seen from the San Antonio street entrance.

[EL PASO PUBLIC LIBRARY]

The State National occupied the old City National Bank building (now Blumenthal building, on Pioneer Plaza) while the white marble edifice was being built on San Antonio street in 1921.

[EL PASO PUBLIC LIBRARY]

Many prominent El Pasoans belonged to the Toltec Club, a social organization of considerable esteem. This group assembled at Washington Park for a baseball game in the early 1900s. By the number, and counter-clockwise: 1. Charles N. Bassett, 2. Winchester Cooley, 3. J. C. Peyton, 4. D. C. Sutton, 5. Bert Semple, 6. Van C. Wilson, 7. B. F. Darbyshire, 8. Otis C. Coles, Sr., 9. Reynolds Coleman, 10. Carl A. Beers, 11. J. L. Dyer. (Carl Beers still resides in El Paso.)

[MRS. H. M. DAUGHERTY, SR.]

The two main buildings of "Texas State College of Mines and Metallurgy" (now The University of Texas at El Paso) soon after it opened in September 1914 on the mesa east of Fort Bliss.

[U.T. EL PASO ARCHIVES]

Construction of The State National's new building, at its second location, began in March 1921 and was completed in eleven months.

[J. E. MORGAN & SONS]

Looking north on Oregon street in 1924 – on the left is The State National, in the far center is the U.S. Court House and on the right is Hotel Essex, where the SNB Motor Bank and Trust Division are now located. [CHRIS P. FOX]

This white marble building, opened in 1922, has been The State National's home for fifty years. The section at right was added on in 1942 and another section, in the rear, was added on in 1948. [M. C. MCKINNEY]

CHARLES N. BASSETT
[MRS. C. N. BASSETT]

GEORGE M. FLORY
[MISS CONSTANCE PATEMAN]

ROBERT W. MCAFEE
[EL PASO HERALD-POST]

The State National Motorbank on Oregon street, since 1954.

[M. G. MCKINNEY]

Groundbreaking ceremony for the new bank building as seen from the Bassett Tower, January 30, 1970.

[M. G. MCKINNEY]

EMPLOYEES WITH MORE THAN THIRTY YEARS SERVICE

From left, standing: ROBERT E. AUSTIN, *Vice President;* FRED K. HUBER, *Vice President and Trust Auditor;* G. FREEMAN HARRIS, *Vice President;* WILLIAM W. PARK, *Assistant Vice President;* SIDNEY W. HOWARD, *Vice President and Cashier;* E. BERT NEUGEBAUER, *Vice President;* JAMES H. ALCORN, *Vice President. Seated:* WILLIAM F. HANLEY, *Vice President;* JACK W. CLARK, *Vice President and Trust Officer;* JACK MOORE, *Vice President;* BOWMAN LIVINGSTON, *Assistant Vice President;* CHARLES D. MCKAY, *Vice President.*

Other 30-year veterans are GEORGE G. MATKIN, H. M. DAUGHERTY, SR., WALTER W. SCOTT *and* E. GUYLER MAGRUDER, *pictured opposite page 150.*

$102,939.91 for the half year ending on January 1, 1920. They stood at $245,698.35 on January 1, 1925.[7]

The financial stresses of the Twenties never seriously affected the prosperity of The State National Bank. For a number of reasons, including its remoteness from the big money markets, El Paso was slow to react to depressive influences and the effects were apt to be less drastic than elsewhere. About the only evidence of the 1924 recession in the bank's records is a reduction from four to three percent in interest rates on savings and certificates of deposit.

The hazards of the early twenties, however, were not all financial. The social stresses and strains were just as dangerous, and El Paso suffered severely from some of them. Beginning in 1921, the town was divided as it never was before and never has been since by the activities of the Ku Klux Klan. The gangsterism and disrespect for law which followed the passage of the eighteenth amendment persuaded many good people that drastic measures were needed, and the Klan, with its program of "native, white, protestant supremacy" and its call for renewed "Chivalry, Humanity, Justice and Patriotism" seemed to many religious, public-spirited, conscientious people to provide the answer. They accepted the secrecy, the racial and religious prejudice and the strong-arm methods of the group as necessary under the circumstances. In July of 1921, Frontier Klan No. 11, Knights of the Ku Klux Klan of the City of El Paso, was organized. Crosses began to burn on Mount Franklin.

Lawyers, doctors, preachers, business leaders joined. In a letter to the *Times* on November 4, 1921, one of them estimated that the aggregate worth of the membership was sixteen million dollars.

The opposing faction was made up of men who were completely horrified at the thought of turning El Paso over to night riders, masked vigilantes, and secret tribunals but they were just as willing as the Klansmen to use violence. More than once, when the Klan announced that it was going to parade, a serious civil disturbance was barely averted. Editor James S. Black of the *Times* (whose life had been threatened because he opposed the Invisible Empire) called the city "an armed camp."[8]

Masons were forbidden to join the Klan, but a great many Masons belonged, and the leaders wanted more. Two of them came to Walter Scott at The State National Bank and urged him to enlist. "You want me because I am Worshipful Master of my lodge," he told them. "Thank you. I'm not interested."

George Matkin, still not much more than a boy and never a joiner, found out what was going on when a man who did a good deal of printing for the bank asked him to come to the office. George went, and listened with some consternation to an offer of membership in the Klan. Embarrassed and troubled, he replied that he didn't think he would be interested.

"Well, you will just have to choose," said the older man. "In six months you are going to have to be for us or against us."

It came to that even sooner than either of them expected. George Flory called the staff together and laid it on the line: "Anybody who joins the Klan has no place in this bank and his connection will be terminated automatically."

It was a courageous act — one certain to alienate a good many influential people — but Bassett, Flory, and the other officers had never been compromisers and did not propose to shilly-shally now. They lost a few accounts and a few employees but in the long run they were justified.[9]

Through 1922 the Klan had almost everything its own way. It may have enrolled as many as 3,500 members and its influence was felt in every corner of the city's affairs. The school board was controlled by Klansmen. The Grand Jury in 1922 included only two men who were not members. By 1923, however, the Klan was on the way out and gradually lost its influence.

The end of the twenties brought trouble of a different kind. When the tide of speculation in stocks and securities began to rise in 1928, building up to the crash of October, 1929, Bassett and Flory were cautious as usual and refused to endanger the bank by extending too much credit to speculators. It was not easy to hold back at a time like this but Mr. Flory not merely tried to protect his own business; he urged his friends and associates to be wary likewise. Guyler Magruder heard him on the telephone one time talking to a close friend and customer who had made a lot of money and was now playing the stock market. Mr. Flory was being very earnest with him. "Now listen," he said, "I want you to sell off enough of that stock to pay off all your debts, buy yourself a half million dollars worth of Liberty Bonds, and then you can play with the balance."

The man replied, "George, you are a damn fool. I'm making ten thousand dollars a day in that market."

"In two months," Magruder remembers, "He was broke. Still owed on his house. But I have a very fine remembrance of that man. He went back into business and paid off everybody. It took him several years. Every few weeks he would bring me a check when I was in the collection cage and I'd pro rate it out to all his creditors. It would be a different amount every time, but he paid them all off. And ended up a rich man — left a nice estate.

"It gave me an insight into people and character. Ninety-nine plus percent of people will pay you if you make it possible. I see them come into the bank even today — people who had to have notes charged off back there, and they went to work and paid them off.

"I remember a fellow named Gaines. He owed a thousand dollars and paid it off in five-and-ten-dollar-a-month payments. And *he* kept track of the interest and paid that off too. Many others did the same thing.

"It was a beautiful thing to see: people who were really broke, and they'd pay off. We could have foreclosed on a lot of them. I'll give you an example about Mr. Flory. This old fellow named Brown had the Finnegan-Brown Hide Company here (we called him Hidehouse Brown). He owed us $2,500. He walked into Mr. Flory's office and said, 'I'm broke, George,' and he hands Flory a deed to his house. He was quite old. His little old house, out in Government Hill, wasn't worth more than $2,500. He said, 'I don't want you to lose any money, and there's a deed to my house. It's yours. Deeded to The State National Bank. I won't need it much longer.' Mr. Flory had the note brought in, stamped it paid, like that, handed it to him, and tore the deed up. Mr. Brown was right about not needing it very long. He died about a year later."[10]

In these affairs the ending was not always happy. One El Paso businessman who wanted to borrow fifty thousand dollars to buy stocks was refused by Mr. Flory for what he considered good and sufficient reason. "He got mad," Magruder recollects, "and pulled his account out of here. Even after the market crashed, he was mad. I went over to see him, and I said, 'I still have that list of stock you wanted to buy.' The fifty thousand dollars was now down to eight thousand on the market. I said, 'Mr. Flory *saved* you forty-two thousand dollars.'

" 'I don't give a damn. He turned me down!' And he wouldn't have anything to do with this bank till Mr. Flory died."

Mr. Flory was not all heart. He could be tough enough when the occasion seemed to him to call for it. But he had as much heart as a banker could afford, and maybe a little bit more.

It was his courage and diligence and foresight, along with the dedication and patience of his officers, that pulled the bank through the hard times. The hardest of all came in 1931, but the men at the State National saw it coming and were ready for it when it arrived.

The twenties were dangerous years for banks in El Paso. In 1920 eleven of them were functioning. Twelve years later the State National was the only survivor, although the El Paso National Bank, organized in 1925, was by then very much in the picture. In the alternating boom and depression years after 1921, with agriculture in difficulties and ranch loans going bad, only capable, experienced, tough-minded bankers had much chance of survival. The natural thing for a bank in trouble was to take chances, hoping for a break. The next step was to merge with another bank, also in precarious condition. As things usually turned out, such a merger did more harm than good and there was another failure. In the twenties, for instance, the El Paso Bank and Trust Company merged with the Rio Grande Bank and Trust Company. This combination then merged with the City National Bank, which closed its doors in 1924. Most of the business handled by the City National came to the State National, which was considered (and certainly was) the soundest bank in El Paso. Some fine employees came with the business, notably Bill Hanley and Jack W. Clark (now vice-presidents) and Evie Van de Water (now Mrs. W. W. Wimberly), who was in charge of Safety Deposit when she retired.

Following the pattern set by the three banks just mentioned, the Security Bank and Trust and the Commercial Bank and Trust Company combined and then merged with the Border National

Bank to become the National Border Bank. It didn't work. The doors had to close.[11] And more business came to the State National along with Bert Neugebauer, now a vice president. State Bank Examiner Sam D. Young took charge of the defunct institutions, joined forces with C. M. Harvey of the Security Trust and Savings, and bought their assets. In 1925 they started the El Paso National Bank.

The proud and prestigious First National went the way of its predecessors. For many years it was the big bank in El Paso with an aggressive management which did business with a good deal of flourish. Joshua Raynolds, the founder, had several banks and many other business connections, mostly in New Mexico. James McNary, his son-in-law and El Paso representative, was a charming extrovert with extraordinary musical talent. He was a singer and conductor; his wife was a fine organist. Together they did a great deal for serious music in the border city. They were social pace setters also and built a house in Austin Terrace (it is a Franciscan seminary now) which was the show place of the town. McNary was not running the bank in 1931 but the seeds of trouble were planted during his time as president and he had to take a good deal of blame for what happened.

The First National and the First Mortgage Company, which was connected with it, were behind some spectacular developments like the great Circle Cross Ranch, started about 1914, which once stretched from the Mescalero Reservation almost as far south as Ysleta and took in a million acres. Oliver Lee, whose name is still a legend in the Tularosa Country, was manager; James McNary was president. Drought and falling prices eventually broke the ranch, but even before this happened, the First National was in trouble. In 1931 it had combined with other banks – a sure sign of weakness – and was actually four banks: the Union Bank and Trust Company, The Manhattan Bank and Trust Company, the Texas Bank and Trust Company, plus the First National itself. Mr. Flory knew what was happening. He used to say that the First National had failed long before the worst happened.[12]

The advent of the Great Depression brought disaster. Through 1929 and 1930 business had been close to normal. We had no hobo jungles and apple peddlers, bread lines and soup kitchens – not yet. But by the fall of 1931 things were beginning to tighten up. Fewer teachers were hired by the public schools, though there were more children to teach. When the gas company insisted on full payment of bills, refusing to accept partial payment, there was much public indignation. H. S. Hunter printed in his "Around Here" column in the *Times* a letter from a thirty-five-year-old ex-serviceman with a wife and child. In fifteen months he had had four months of work. "All I want is a job," he said. "I am not afraid of work. All I want is a chance."[13]

His words were an echo of what was being said all over the country. Hard times were here, the worst the land had ever seen, and business slowed to a standstill. A total of 1345 banks failed in 1930 and bank holidays were declared by several governors. Uneasiness was universal. When whispers began to circulate about the First National, people started withdrawing their money, and it looked to President F. M. Murchison as if a run were in the making. With $1,500,000 in cash on hand and $1,600,000 in paper (his figures), he decided that he couldn't pay off if a run actually started. On Friday, September 4, ten minutes before the ten-o'clock opening time, a notice appeared on the door of the bank, advising the public that the First National would not open.[14]

By the time the notice went up, a crowd had already gathered in the street, and it grew steadily. The morning was warm, and the men drifted across to the shade in front of the State National. The bank was open for business, of course, and customers were going in and out. One or two at a time, worried depositors detached themselves from the restless assembly on the street corner and lined up in front of the two paying-tellers. Before you could say "Money," the State National had a full-fledged run on its hands.

Panic is a contagious thing. Hysteria spread through the crowd like a cold wave. The men fought and shoved each other, trying to get up to the cages, and the look on their faces was fearful to see.

"It scared hell out of me," says Bert Neugebauer, "and everybody else. There were a few wet spots on the floor, too. I'll never forget it."[15]

Mr. Flory was loaded for a run. He had great bundles of bills stacked up in the cages where they could easily be seen. He put

Forrest Smith and Guyler Magruder, two of his fastest tellers, on the job and told them to pay it out. Each one had a girl behind him looking up the accounts while he handed out the money. Working as fast as they could, they got rid of about $800,000 that first awful day. The run continued into the next day, and they got rid of a good deal more.

When the excitement was at its height, Mr. Flory came out of his office and attempted to calm the crowd down. "Take your time. Don't hurry. Your money is here and you're going to get it." Nothing he could say seemed to make any difference. The crush went on. The tellers drank cokes and ate sandwiches and stayed on the job hour after hour, counting the money and shoving it into the outstretched, grasping hands.[16]

In making his preparations, Flory had thought in terms of everyday business and was well stocked with small-sized bills – ones and fives and tens and twenties. He realized almost at once, however, that what he needed was hundreds, five hundreds, and thousands. He pulled Hal Daugherty out of the paying cage and started him on a series of trips to the Federal Reserve Bank exchanging small bills for large ones. "All right," he rasped, "you get the Cop Car and go down there and bring $300,000 on every trip. That's all our insurance will cover."

"I spent the day doing it," Hal says. "You didn't turn a thing like that over to a messenger. There were no armored cars in town in those days. We would make a contribution to the policeman's pension fund – twenty-five dollars a month – and they would send a car when we needed it. There was some criticism about it later on."[17]

Bigger bills speeded things up some. "I never will forget," Guyler Magruder recalls, "this guy came in – a Frenchman – had a check for $50,000. I counted out his money, including some thousand-dollar bills, just like that. I haven't seen a thousand-dollar bill since. The next day he tried to put it back and Mr. Flory wouldn't take it."

Quite understandably Mr. Flory didn't like what was going on and he showed his irritation. When one man tried to cash a check for $900, the teller turned around to look at the ledger and found that he had $916 in the bank. Mr. Flory was watching and saw the situation. He scratched out the $900 and wrote in $916. "Give him all his money," he said, "and get him out of here. If he doesn't want his money in this bank, I don't want him around."[18]

There were a few lighter moments. Evie Van de Water Wimberly tells about one. "I was in savings," she says, "and we paid out a lot of money. Savings is the first hit when a run is started. The lines were long and the checks were big. A tall young Negro woman was standing in line. She didn't push. She didn't hurry. When she got to my window, she said, 'I'd like to make a deposit.' She looked around at the crowd and said, 'Ma'am, business is sure good.' "

They closed at five – the regular hour – because of necessity. All those transactions had to be put on the books, and it took till three the next morning to do it. On Saturday, business was supposed to be over at twelve, but when noon arrived, the lobby was still jammed with frightened people. Mr. A. Schwartz of the Popular Dry Goods Company happened in at that moment and made his way to Mr. Flory's office.

"What are you going to do, George?" he asked.

"We are going to stay open as long as any customer is waiting to be served."

"In that case, you'd better put up some notices in the lobby to tell these people so. I have a very good painter that can fix up the signs right away." And the ever-helpful Mr. Schwartz went off to see about it.

By one o'clock the announcements were in place: the bank would stay open as long as anybody wanted to do business. Fifteen minutes later the lobby was almost empty. The run was broken.[19]

In the Sunday *Times* Mr. Flory announced to those who might be interested that although Monday was Labor Day, the bank would be open from eight to five.

At eight o'clock Monday the staff was on hand and exceptionally busy, but this time they were not paying out money – they were taking it in. All the officers went at the job of making out deposit slips for new accounts. Working at top speed, they wrote out the slips and threw them into big wastebaskets on the floor. When a basket was full, they sent it off, hoping the figures would check.

A good deal of the business that would have gone to the First National was coming into the State National, and a small mountain of papers accumulated around everybody but the janitor. It took days and nights of steady work to get it all processed, but the staff was ready for that too. George Matkin, in charge of personnel, took on additional help and the *esprit de corps* of the State National did the rest. Nobody watched the clock or worried too much about meals or sleep. The job was there to do, and they did it.

The fall of the First National was a real calamity and it cut deeply into the morale of the town. A sort of chain reaction set in. The First National Bank of Las Cruces, a corresponding bank of the El Paso institution, closed its doors. It was in no danger, according to President W. P. B. McSain, who declared that he would reopen "when the hysteria ends."[20] He kept his promise, but he stayed closed for several months. The First Mortgage Company, which had connections with the First National Bank, failed within the year. Business in the El Paso trade area slowed down to a crawl.

There was some hope of reopening the First National. Businessmen tried hard to raise the million dollars it would take to set the bank back on its feet, but everybody was afraid and the attempt failed. In due time depositors were paid off at the rate of about fifty cents on the dollar, but all assets including the bank fixtures were sold and the main lobby of the old bank became an echoing cavern, deserted except for an occasional bazaar or theatrical performance, until J. B. Blaugrund bought it and made it the home of the American Furniture Company.

New business which came to the State National after the crash made it necessary to employ more people and enlarge its working space. The original structure, 122 by 48 feet, was adequate in 1922, but not in 1932. To make more room, the bank rented the adjoining property from Mrs. Ida Pfaff and eventually bought it. Two other purchases at the rear brought the bank's quarters to their ultimate proportions, but that, of course, came later.

And so the crisis of 1931 was successfully weathered, but the Depression was just beginning in the Southwest, and more dark days were ahead.

CHAPTER VIII

MR. FLORY'S BOYS

• FOR FIFTEEN YEARS George Flory's heart had given him trouble, and by 1930 he knew his time was running out. He was not one to worry or complain about it, but he did begin to try to squeeze a little more juice out of life. After all those years in the bachelor establishment on San Antonio Street, he and Maury Edwards decided that they ought to have a house. They bought a lot on Blacker Street on the mesa — the high ground north of town — behind Rim Road and got a great deal of pleasure out of watching the blueprints become brick-and-plaster reality.

"We wanted a nice place to live while we last," Edwards remarked one time when a friend inquired what they had in mind, at their age, in building such a fine large dwelling. "We won't last long."[1]

Only the best in materials and workmanship would do, and the house was built like a battleship. There are no cracks in the walls today.[2] It was planned for male living, not for entertaining and showing off, but it had to have curtains and bathroom fixtures and wall paper. Mr. Flory enjoyed asking the girls at the bank for their opinion about this item or that — which tile should go in what bathroom — and they loved participating in his belated dream. When all was finished, he invited everybody in the bank to an open house.

Not very long after he moved in, the First National failed and the State National survived the run. It was the climax of George Flory's career as a banker and the last big scene in which he played a part.

As his health grew worse, he gave up some of his responsibilities, but he never stopped running the bank. Daytimes he was always there and even at night he often came in to see that all was well. He spent as much time out of his office as in it, prowling about to check on bank operations, answering a question here, greeting a customer there, pulling out the two-inch stub pencil he always carried in his vest pocket for impromptu figuring, leaning against a door jamb to scratch his back.

Employees dreaded the thought of crossing him, but they all felt free to ask him for help. "Oh, Mr. Flory," Evie Van de Water would say, "I'm so worried. One of my books is out of balance and I can't find it." And Mr. Flory would turn to and help her locate the mistake.[3]

"The first time I met Mr. Flory, to talk to him," Bert Neugebauer says, "I was out of balance. He kept pretty close to that. He didn't think there was any excuse to be out of balance. He called me into the office, and I was shaking like a leaf, but when he opened his mouth, I just sat there relaxed. He was really some person. Outside he was gruff, but I loved him from that day on."[4]

The Bassett girls adored him and invaded his office when they were downtown, hoping to be taken to lunch. Myra, the eldest, now Mrs. H. M. Daugherty, would come charging into the lobby and crash through the wooden gate that fenced off the offices occupied by Bassett and Flory, calling "George, George!" while all the employees watched with broad smiles.[5] Her younger sisters Barbara (Mrs. Hugh McGovern later) and Betty (now Mrs. Charles B. Hammond) were just as devoted to him.

When he had no other engagement, Mr. Flory ate lunch in his office and sometimes dozed off in his chair. Once while catching a few winks he leaned back too far and fell over with a crash which startled everybody in the bank.

This was long before the wage-and-hour laws, and "overtime" had not become a part of the vocabulary of bookkeepers. People worked as late as necessary to keep up with what had to be done. For bank personnel the last two days in the month were the worst. "Preparatory Night" came first and "Statement Night" was the finale. On those nights everybody worked late – till nine, ten, eleven, twelve. Since December 31 was the last day of the month, the entire staff worked late on New Year's Eve and missed most of the parties.[6]

On the two big nights each person was given a dollar for supper money and ate wherever he liked. It was easy to linger over coffee, however, and the dinner hour expanded little by little until Mr. McAfee, with Mr. Flory's blessing, did something about it. He instructed George Simpson at the Gateway Coffee Shop to serve each employee a steak dinner, which he ate and signed for.[7]

Statement night, surprisingly enough, was actually a fun occasion. Groups of men took their wives and girl friends to Juarez and made a night of it, almost always finishing with food and drink at the Modern Cafe under the Mills Building.[8]

Flory was generous in many ways to his people. As Thanksgiving drew near, he arranged to have a turkey delivered to every employee with a family – a custom which was continued until one of the women complained that she had been discriminated against; that she had been given a small turkey even though Mr. Flory well knew that she had a large family. After that there were no more turkeys, but every year there was a Christmas bonus, not large, but very helpful. Always there was a feeling that Mr. Flory and Mr. Bassett were men of great good will, and their doors and their ears were open to anyone with a reasonable request. The young men they hired were mostly just out of high school, in need of correction and encouragement and advice, and Mr. Flory and Mr. Bassett were part father, part schoolmaster, and occasionally part truant officer in their relationship with these boys.

George Matkin remembers with particular pride that Mr. Flory accepted an appointment as his guardian. George was alone in the world when his mother died, and in order to pay the funeral expenses, he had to have his "disabilities" removed. Someone had to appear as his guardian in court in order to make the request for removal in proper form, and thus George Matkin became the ward of George Flory.

A few days after the relationship was made official, young Matkin appeared in Flory's office smoking a cigarette. Flory looked up with a frown and growled at him, "If I am going to be your father, you will have to take that damn cigarette out of your face."

Flory himself smoked constantly.

The special understanding between Mr. Flory and his boys began with the first interview. He did not like to talk about salary. "You just come in here and make yourself a banker," he would say to the trembling youngster. "Your money will come to you, more than you deserve."

"It did, too," they will assure you today.

The idea of the importance of the job and the secondary significance of the size of the pay check was something Mr. Flory always stressed. It helped to start some fine young men on the road to becoming dedicated and efficient bankers, some of them top officers in the bank today.

Naturally these young men had health, high spirits, energy, and enthusiasm. If they were short on anything, it was inhibitions. "We had a bunch of wild Indians back there," says Jack Clark. Some were wilder than others, but all were close to Mr. Flory's heart. He understood them, bore with them, and loved them. They were his joy and his cross. He would threaten to whip them with a wet rope, but he never failed to come to their defense when they needed him. And boys like Guyler Magruder, Johnny Williams, Bruce Smith, Bob Stewart and Malcolm Webb were apt to need him any time.

They used the bank as a sort of club house. They had keys, of course, and could come in after hours and amuse themselves one way or another. During Prohibition they regarded drinking as an obligation and did a good deal of it. Before dates, they would come by the bank and build up a little enthusiasm. At one time they developed a passion for shooting craps. This was safe enough until they began to slip off to the basement during the daytime. Walter Scott caught them down on their knees one time and threw the dice in the furnace.[8]

More than once Mr. Flory was called on to get them out of trouble. A story still told by the men who remember back that far begins late one afternoon when several of the gang emerged from the side door of the bank with dinner on their minds. Across the street a young woman of minimal or non-existent virtue, sitting conspicuously in a window, called out an invitation to the boys to come up and see her. Webb, an unusually plain-spoken youth, told her what she could do with herself and she called the police, reporting that the boys had insulted her. In a matter of minutes a Black Maria was on the scene and the boys – all of them – were hustled off to jail. Bill Greet, the policeman who was everybody's friend in need, was not to be found so Magruder asked the booking officer to call Mr. Flory. The following interchange ensued:

"Is this Mr. George Flory?"

"Yes, this is George Flory."

"Well, I've got five of your boys down at the city jail."

"How do you know they are my boys?"

"Well, they say they are."

"Are they drunk?"

"No, they're not drunk."

"Then they're not *my* boys!"

There was some pathos in this remark. Mr. Flory implied that his boys drank entirely too much and too often. But without hesitation he called Maury Kemp, a director and one of the bank's attorneys, who came down and took charge. The accused got off with five-dollar fines.[9]

Another time a notorious madam came bustling into the lobby of the bank, snorting and fuming and demanding justice. According to her, some of the same gang had descended upon her place, raised a good deal of hell, and concluded by kicking a door down. She got to Mr. Flory and presented her case with volume and emphasis. Mr. Flory listened, and when she paused, he told her: "You run a house, don't you? Well, you expect to get a door kicked down every now and then. You're not supposed to come in here and bother my boys." And that was all she got out of him.[10]

The worst scandal was strictly intramural. Nobody ever knew of it outside the bank, which was just as well. The trouble began when the boys started having mixed parties there. There was a watchman who should have put a stop to it, but you could give him a dollar and he would find something to keep him busy on the other side of town. So the parties got bigger and better. The focus of activity seemed to be the ladies' room near Safe Deposit downstair where there was a big leather couch. It became obvious eventually to one of the good ladies upstairs that something was going on down there after hours. She fussed about it but got nowhere until one of the boys was careless and left concrete proof of his irregularities on the floor. So George Matkin, then an assistant cashier, was called down to look at what those nasty, filthy boys were doing in her department. Matkin assembled everybody who might have been involved and made inquiries but nobody would admit a thing. One of them, usually the ringleader, said to Matkin, "Well, goddam it, why didn't you come down and join us? You knew what was going on."[11]

Nobody was punished, but there were no more parties.

In those days money was scarce, particularly for young employees, and everybody was always short. The bank allowed officers to borrow up to $2,500 and most of them, at least occasionally, had to ask for loans to tide them over until payday. Ordinary employees were not given these privileges, however, and found it much harder to raise a few dollars. This fact led to the birth of the Gilt Edge Security Company.

Bookkeeper Kenneth Gifford was the financier. The usual formula was "Six for Five till Payday," but as time went on, the deals became larger and more complicated. The crapshooting down in the furnace room was part of it. Stakes got higher and higher and the losers began to pass out IOU's. Among the gamblers was a boy who owned a Chrysler convertible – new model, with soft tires and everything up to date. Gifford had a mortgage on it, but when the owner was caught short in the crap game, he put up the title to his car to stay in. He lost again, and Gifford got ready to make a serious objection.

About that time one of the junior officers approached Gifford and wanted to borrow a thousand dollars. "Eight per cent," he said.

"No, hell with you. Twelve percent's the rate," Gifford told him.

"Hell with you. I'm going to the old man about it."

So Mr. Flory found out about the crap game and the Chrysler convertible and the Gilt Edge Security Company.

Gifford laughs about it now: " 'How long has this been going on?' Mr. Flory asked, and his eyes got that big. So the Gilt Edge Security Company went into liquidation that afternoon and I moved my affairs outside the bank." The formation of Mr. Gifford's Finance Trust Company was the direct result.[12]

It would be unfair to record only these anecdotes about Mr. Flory's boys. His confidence in them was not misplaced. Some went into other businesses but many of them stayed with the bank, or returned to it after trying out other jobs, and did much useful service. New ideas and procedures were apt to proceed from their shrewd and fertile minds.

There was the matter of installment loans, for instance. "We didn't make an installment loan in this bank until 1936," says Guyler Magruder. "We had to wait for an Italian named Giannini, who started the Bank of Italy in San Francisco, to revolutionize the banking industry by lending to poor people. You would make provision for a loan, and you'd deposit in Savings every month, and when your savings equaled the loan, it was paid off. That was the way they set it up."[13] When the officers came to the conclusion that the bank should have a Personal Loan Department, Mr. Bassett agreed, but he was frankly skeptical. "I don't want it in the bank," he said. "Put it down in the basement." So Mr. Robert F. Youngberg went downstairs and took charge of the new service.

It was the same with automobile loans. Mr. Bassett was temperamentally opposed to such things. "If a man doesn't have the money to pay for a car, he ought not to buy it," he would say. "They aren't very good anyway. They wear out. I'm against it." Some of the younger officers, notably George Matkin, were in favor of lending money on automobiles, but for a long time the bank was wary of such loans except through dealers. The wheels of progress turned, however, as often as not because one of Mr. Flory's boys had a bright idea. He encouraged them to use their minds, and in return they gave him a respect and devotion which they gave nobody else. When you hear them talk about him today, you know they are still his boys, even though he was always on their backs about something.

One thing he constantly deviled them about was waste. Like Mr. Morehead in his day, he was outraged to find a light burning in the basement when nobody was around to use it. He said to Kenneth Gifford (this was before the Gilt Edge Security Company folded), "You haven't got anything to do. Why the hell don't you see that those lights are turned out?" The upshot was that Kenneth would be watching, and when Mr. Flory came out of his office for his regular swing around by the water fountain and downstairs, the Gifford desk would be vacant and Kenneth would be on his way to check the lights. "The vault had a kind of dog leg in it," he recalls, "and you couldn't see the back light. Once I turned off the light in the outer vault near the hallway, but I didn't know this other one was burning. So he went by and found it, and he ate me out about that.

"Jack Moore and I were bookkeepers in those days, and he and his gang wanted to make it nice for me, so they went out and bought a 500-watt bulb. Of course we couldn't afford to have anything but fifties around the bank. That was all you could have. That was big enough. So they put that 500-watt bulb in the back vault so somebody would go back there and turn it on and leave it, and I would catch the devil. George Flory did find that big light back there and like to had a fit. But there wasn't anybody that knew anything about it at all."[14]

These teapot tempests were only a small part of George Flory's life. In those last years he found much to enjoy. He located some relatives back in Maryland – went back to see them – gave them wonderful presents at Christmas. They included a mother and several girls and he sent them big boxes of things that girls would enjoy – first letting the women at the bank look his purchases over and make suggestions. The relatives seem to have lived on a farm, for they sent him such things as hams and cakes. The girls in the bank always got the cakes.[15]

His adopted family – the Bassett girls – received all the attention he could give them. They went for rides every Sunday in the old touring car that Mr. Bassett had turned over to him, and they always stopped somewhere for refreshments. He used all his ingenuity to find different and interesting Christmas presents for them. For a while he gave them white doeskin trousers and coats and shirts made by the Indians somewhere. When they asked him what they were going to get, however, he would say, "Nothing, absolutely nothing! This Christmas I'm going to give the things I've bought to some little girls down town who don't have as much as you do."[16] But they knew better, and he knew that they knew better, and they knew he knew that they knew better. It was a wonderful relationship.

Early in 1932 his condition grew serious. He went off to Johns

Hopkins Hospital and underwent treatment, including some sort of surgery, and came home improved. On Friday, June 10, he got up at two in the morning to go hunting with Maury Edwards – something he loved to do – and perhaps he overdid. On Monday he collapsed. Dr. W. L. Brown was called. Charley Bassett, almost down himself with rheumatism, stayed at the bedside hoping for improvement, but George Flory had finished his course. He slipped farther and farther into the quiet world where his old friends could not follow him and from which he could not return.[17] Mrs. Harmon, a friend of the family, took the Bassett girls up to Cloudcroft to ease the shock of losing the man who meant so much to them. At five in the morning of June 14, George Flory began the long journey.

"The city is poorer for losing him," said the *Times* editorial writer. It was the least that could be said of such a man. The city had indeed lost a fine citizen. Sick and crippled children had lost one of their two best friends (C. N. Bassett was the other). The bank had lost a firm hand on the controls. And Mr. Flory's boys were without their strongest ally and most trustworthy guide. Ask any one of them today and he will tell you so.

Chapter IX

BANK HOLIDAY

• George Flory's death in June, 1932, took him out of a world in which everybody was finding it harder and harder to live. While the officers of The State National Bank were carrying him to his final resting place, the Bonus Army was camping in Washington and the Hoover Administration was trying desperately to find solutions for insoluble problems. The National Credit Corporation was created in the fall of 1931 to reduce the strain on weak banks throughout the nation, and the Reconstruction Finance Corporation moved into the action early in 1932.[1] The country was too far gone to be saved by such measures. After a brief upswing in the summer of 1932, the mood of discouragement and distrust gripped the country once more.

Cash money—coins for telephone calls and shoeshines and newspapers and items at the grocery store – was unbelievably scarce. Cities in the South began to print their own currency and Hoover called on all citizens to give up the practice of hoarding. They ignored him and went on withdrawing their savings from every bank in the land, convinced that their money was safer in a mattress or a cookie jar in the pantry, or even buried out in the back yard. By the end of Mr. Hoover's term in office, $1,212,000,000 had been withdrawn from circulation.

The banking system could not stand the strain. Between 1930 and 1932, 773 national banks and 3604 state banks failed with deposits totaling billions.[2]

Misery followed in the wake of financial paralysis. In 1932 more than thirteen million men were unemployed. A million, perhaps two million, of these men were on the road looking for jobs, just moving along because there was nothing else to do. The freight cars passing through El Paso were loaded with them. The park benches in the plaza provided sleeping quarters for them every night.

Unemployment began to be a local problem in 1931 as the failure of the First National sapped public confidence and slowed the already faltering economy. Jobs were harder and harder to find. On October 20 a woman fainted on the street. She had been thirty hours without food.

J. R. Martin of the Government Employment Bureau announced in September that 7,000 unemployed men had registered in El Paso and estimated that 2,000 more had not registered. Repercussions were felt all the way out to the campus of the College of Mines. Coach Mack Saxon was gloomy about football prospects. There will be no team, he said, "unless athletes can find jobs." Four good players were already lost.[3]

A plague of hoboes struck the town and panhandling on the streets expanded to include city-wide back-door begging. The *Times* noted that the chief of police at Prescott, Arizona, had threatened to put all the hoboes in his town on the chain gang. "That's no threat," said H. S. Hunter in his "Around Here" column. "It's a promise. Plenty of men would welcome chain gang work on the streets to get food and a bed."[4]

Everybody was concerned about the situation. Those who were able did something about it. C. N. Bassett instructed George Simpson to set up a soup dispensary at the back door of the Gateway Coffee Shop (Mr. Bassett owned the Gateway Hotel) and George did so, providing meals for a surprising number of hungry human beings. Every week Mr. Bassett sent a check to the coffee shop to cover the cost of the soup.

El Paso did what it could for its own. The county bought 3,000 acres in McKelligon Canyon for $30,000 and put men to work on emergency flood-control projects. A bond issue to finance this work was bitterly opposed by many influential citizens, but when the chips were down they passed it rather than stop the work and bring a thousand men closer to starvation.[5]

The citizens who opposed the bond issue had one good point. There was a great shortage of cotton pickers in the Valley, and nobody wanted to work for wages the farmers could afford to pay. Not until the police began to make arrests for vagrancy ("Pick cotton or get out of town") and the county commissioners cut off support for the Salvation Army's kitchen did the situation change.

By October 14, however, J. R. Martin was moving 350 men a day to the farms.[6]

Roosevelt crushed Hoover in the November elections, and the last months of the Republican administration were the most difficult of all. Roosevelt held aloof, rejecting Hoover's pleas for a joint effort at restoring confidence and business activity. The government nevertheless did its best to organize relief on a national scale. The RFC set up an office in El Paso in February, 1932, with E. W. Kayser, late of the First National bank, in charge, and money began to trickle into the community – not enough to solve many problems but enough to keep destitute people alive. Direct relief, according to published figures, had gone to 4259 families – 17,000 persons – by December of 1932. The Salvation Army, with an insignificant subsidy, had assisted 1,561 "homeless wanderers."[7]

Nothing the Hoover administration could do, however, had the least effect on the steady decline of the economy. The banking industry continued to disintegrate. On October 31, 1932, Nevada proclaimed a twelve-day bank holiday to save the state's financial existence. In other Western states an epidemic of bank failures erupted.[8] Through the winter months it went on, as Hoovervilles and hobo camps grew, bread lines lengthened, and Americans began to talk about the possibility of revolution.

El Paso got through this difficult time as well as any community in the country. Wages went lower and lower, but so did prices. Even a small income went a long way. The four new Ph. D.'s brought in to strengthen the faculty of the College of Mines in the fall of 1931 made only $1,800 for nine months, and they had to discount their warrants at the State National (the State of Texas was far behind in its payments), but before the Depression was over, one of them had got married, had a baby and taken two trips to Europe. Money went a long way in the thirties.

Some people were, in fact, doing very well. On September 6 H. S. Hunter devoted his "Around Here" column in the *Times* to "The Great Fur Coat Movement." Half the women in town, he declared, had fur coats in layaway. The conclusion is inescapable that some people during the worst days of the Depression were better off than before.

It was the contrast between the arrogance of the haves and the misery of the have-nots that brought many good citizens to a boil, and in their minds the bankers were the villains. There was ample foundation for their disillusion. In April, 1932, an investigation of Wall Street banking practices began, with J. P. Morgan himself on the list of witnesses. The revelations were astonishing and appalling. Few of the titans of finance bothered to pay any income tax. They rigged the market, sold shares to their friends at reduced prices, and unloaded worthless stock on the American public.[9] People had to blame somebody for their troubles, and the bankers began to be universally despised.

As the Hoover administration entered its last days and the final shreds of public confidence were eaten away, the banking system entered what seemed to be its final agony. On February 4 banking activity was suspended in Louisiana. On the fourteenth the Governor of Michigan closed down all the banks in his state. By the first of March Alabama, California, Idaho, Kentucky, Mississippi and Tennessee had followed suit. On March 4, the day of Franklin Roosevelt's inauguration, Governor Lehmann of New York suspended banking operations. The financial system of the United States of America was completely paralyzed when Franklin Roosevelt and Herbert Hoover rode together up Pennsylvania Avenue to inaugurate the New Deal.

In his inaugural address Roosevelt blamed the bankers for what had happened and invoked the wrath of God upon them. He called for an end to "speculation with other people's money" and for "an adequate but sound currency." "The money changers," he said, "have fled from their high seats in the temple of our civilization. We may now restore that temple to its ancient truths. The measure of that restoration lies in the extent to which we apply social values more noble than mere monetary profit."[10]

That was on Saturday, March 4. On Sunday Roosevelt called for a special session of Congress, stopped the export of gold, and proclaimed a national bank holiday.

The banking situation in Texas never quite got to the point of collapse. In fact, banks like the State National were in far better shape than those in the East. It had plenty of money on hand. Late in February George Matkin, then cashier of the State National, had a call from the treasurer of a big company back East — one of his biggest accounts. The man said, "We've got to meet a payroll in our Los Angeles factory. Can you possibly ship the money out there?"

"I'd be delighted," George told him, "and we'd like to have it as part of our records that we've done this to help you. My advice would be that you give me the authorization right now so I can attend to it immediately. The way things are going, we are liable to be in the same position as California." So the executive gave George authorization then and there and the money went off by mail.

At that very moment George was getting ready to go to Austin to attend a meeting called by Governor Miriam Ferguson. She wanted to discuss the situation with the leading bankers of the state and decide what ought to be done. The group was not large, but among the chosen she had placed the name of C. N. Bassett and had called to ask him to come. Mr. Bassett said he was not about to leave town at a time like that, but suggested that George Matkin make the trip. On the week end of the Roosevelt inauguration, George was en route to the meeting.

"I had to take the T & P to Dallas and change trains to get there," he says. "We arrived and I went up to her office. There must have been fifteen bankers in the room. I think I was the youngest one. Most of them were presidents of banks in Houston and Dallas — big banks for those days. We were sitting around waiting for her to call us into her office, and she sent her secretary out to say that the President had just called a national bank holiday. It was out of her hands and we could go back home. She didn't need us. I never even saw her. I got back to El Paso and walked into the bank. The doors were open but no one was at the windows. The boys and girls were sitting around in the work rooms playing bridge and having a good time. It just did something to you to see what was going on."[11]

On Moday the bank had received a telegram informing the staff that until further notice nothing was to be posted and no more checks were to be issued or received.

The officers were not really worried. The bank was in good condition in spite of all that had been happening. Salaries were low, lower than they would have been had Mr. Bassett and his officers not tried to keep as many people as possible on the payroll, but in those times a job was something to be thankful for and there were no complaints. Mr. Flory's shrewdness and foresight were still working for his bank, though he was not there in person to help. Loans were in excellent shape and other assets were flexible. Everybody in the bank knew that the institution was sound. The big difficulty was the uncertainty. Nobody could foresee what would be asked of the staff. And next to that was the fact that while the bank stayed closed, it lost money. Too much delay in reopening might be disastrous.

One big difficulty was the fact that the government could not make up its mind during the first few days of the moratorium. First the instructions said, No Business. Then came a telegram authorizing the employees to post clearings and handle paper already in the bank. "Well, we posted those," says Sidney Howard, "got all the books posted and balanced, and then we got another wire saying no, we couldn't do that. We had to take everything off, so we went back and unposted it all – credited each check back and debited each credit and got that all taken off. And then a day or so later they let us post the stuff back again, so it was a kind of mess for a while. Nobody knew exactly what we were expected to do."[12]

Telegrams came in every day explaining the regulations, setting up new ones, and changing the ones already set up. At the same time the bank officers were in frequent session, trying to live up to the rules and wishing for a lawyer to interpret the language of these communications. A few checks were allowed to go through – for instance when the money was needed to buy medicine for the sick – but there was no cash in circulation to provide for everyday necessities, and the situation could easily have got out of hand. The bank did something about it. George Matkin tells the story:

"On the Saturday after the Bank Holiday began, Mr. Bassett called us into a meeting and said, 'We need some money in this town just so people can buy things that they need to buy. They can get lots of things on credit, but they need some money. I don't care whether it's against the regulations or not, I'm going to open up on Saturday morning and let everybody cash a check for twenty-five dollars.' So we ran a notice in the paper that we were going to do that. We had people come into the bank that we had never seen before and cash a twenty-five-dollar check. They didn't even have an account with us, but we cashed the checks for them. When we opened up after the moratorium, we collected them all. We had no losses. But everybody came in and got twenty-five dollars. I think the El Paso National followed suit and did the same thing.

"I remember a banker friend of mine from up in New Mexico who came to my house a day or two later and said, 'You fellows have got all of my money in my account in your bank, and I can't get it. You've told your customers that they can have twenty-five dollars. What am I going to do? I want to do the same thing.'

"I said, 'All right, you tell me how many accounts you have and I'll get you that much money.'

"So I gave him a bag of money – several thousand dollars. A day or two later he came back with the same bag and handed it to me. He said, 'Not a soul came in to get it. They didn't want any money in my town, so put this back in my account.'

"I said, 'No, I'm not going to do it. You've got it out. I'll just hold this bag as a personal possession of yours in safekeeping so I can give it back to you. If I put it in your account, you'll probably be back in here again wanting it, and maybe I can't give it to you then.'

"So we held that money until the thing was over. And I remember that when we gave him his bag of money again, he broke down and cried, he was so disturbed about the situation.

"I remember particularly the railroads. El Paso had three railroads, and in those days they handled a tremendous amount of freight of all sizes, and they had agents who made up their deposits at certain intervals. The railroad treasurers continued to make deposits as they always had, and we couldn't handle them. We couldn't post them. We couldn't collect them. All we could do was just stack them up. We were forbidden to cash pay checks, and before it was over we were giving the railroads cash to pay their men. We had to keep the railroads running. We took just an ordinary full-size trunk. You don't see trunks any more, but it those days you did. Just an ordinary trunk. We put it in the vault and stacked their deposits in that. The trunk was full before the banking holiday was over.

"We used to wonder how much trouble we were going to have processing and collecting those checks, but not a single one of them was returned. It just went through smoothly and the railroads didn't lose a dime.

"One of the food men said at a Chamber of Commerce meeting that he wasn't going to take any checks. He had good groceries and good food, and if anyone wanted to, he could buy it, but he wasn't going to take a chance.

"Another man told him, 'You're crazy. You've got to feed those people. If you don't, they'll step down there and take it away from you.' He decided to do it, and didn't have any trouble.

"Mr. Schwartz of the Popular came in and said, 'I'm getting all these checks. I want you to post them and credit my account. I don't want any money. I'm perfectly willing to wait till this thing clears itself up, but I want to get those checks into my account instead of in the account of the person who wrote them.' We agreed to do it. Some of the other banks objected, but we did it. Our attitude was, 'We're not cashing any checks. We're just getting our books in better shape for when it's over.' We did many things like that, some in violation of the law. The Federal Government could have prosecuted us for those twenty-five-dollar checks, I think, but we had no trouble. We did not ask permission (they would have refused us if we had) so we did not violate a direct order."[13]

It took less than two weeks – until March 14 – for the bank to reopen. Every banking firm in the country was checked out and those that were in good shape were informed by telegram that they could reopen. The two El Paso banks were proud to be among the first to get the message.

Employees were on call so they could go back to work the moment the word came. They were at their posts every day and spent some time catching up on filing and other routine chores, but the checks were piling up all the time – thousands and thousands of them – and it would take a mighty effort on the part of all hands to get caught up after the long delay.

"The moratorium was lifted, I think, on a Sunday night," says Evie Van de Water Wimberly, "and I happened to be in church. I wasn't called, but I heard about it when I got out. I had some very close friends in the Transit Department, and they were called. They went to the bank immediately and started the flow of business. Those checks had to get going. Forrest Smith said to me the night we received our notice from the Comptroller to open, 'Evie were you ever worried?' And I said, 'Not for one minute! I knew we would get it!' "[14]

CHAPTER X

BETWEEN THE DARK AND THE DAYLIGHT

• THE MIRACULOUS and manifold changes that began in March, 1933, revolutionized many aspects of American life and business – none more so that the banking business. In fact, New Deal reforms began with regulation of the American financial system. The Securities Act was passed before the month of March was out, and along with the Securities-Exchange Act (1934) and the Public-Utility-Holding Act (1935) it put brakes on stock manipulation, deception of the buying public, and free-wheeling financial shenanigans in general. In June the Glass-Steagall Act separated commercial banking and investment banking, set up a system of deposit insurance, and put a curb on loaning money for speculation.[1]

Although these regulations made little difference in the practices of sound, conservative banking institutions like The State National Bank of El Paso, they raised the level of respectability and reliability throughout the industry and all banks profited thereby.

The devaluation of the dollar and the abandonment of the gold standard had a more immediate effect on the local banks. In April of 1933 the government went off the gold standard and the Treasury Department began stockpiling both gold and silver. All the gold in circulation was called in.

This meant the breaking of some long-standing habits. Gold coins were preferred currency in El Paso business circles. When Guyler Magruder went to work for the bank in 1920, Mr. Flory, as usual, kept him in the dark about the amount of his salary. At the end of the first month he was handed three twenty-dollar gold pieces.[2] Bank employees were usually paid in gold. After 1933, however, the clink of coins was replaced by the crisp crackle of bills.

Another interesting development was the loss of the bank's gold hoard. One of Mr. Bassett's little hobbies was collecting Indian-head two-and-a-half-dollar gold pieces. He started saving them early in his career as a banker. When a teller received one, he would lay it aside and it would eventually find its way to a special spot in the vault. This went on until the bank had accumulated 3,800 of them – every one a collector's item. Then came the order to turn in all gold coins.

Cashier George Matkin could not bring himself to break up this wonderful and valuable hoard without a protest. He sat down and wrote a personal letter to Secretary of the Treasury Woodin explaining the situation and asking for a special dispensation allowing the bank to keep its stock of Indian-head gold pieces.

"He wrote me a letter," Matkin says; "told me he was a coin collector himself and agreed that they should not be turned in. 'You just put this letter with them,' he wrote, 'so the examiners can see that you have my authority to keep them.'

"So we kept them till Mr. Woodin retired. His successor sent us a telegram about two pages long telling us to turn those two-and-a half-dollar gold pieces in. He had been looking over what Mr. Woodin had been doing and was now doing the opposite. We refused to do it, and every day for about a week we got a long telegram.

"Finally, Mr. Bassett said, 'George, go on and turn them in,' and I said, 'I'm not going to do it.' He said, 'Yes, you're going to have to, so go on and do it.'

"In the days when we had gold, we'd send it to the Federal Reserve just as we send currency now, but they didn't count it. They weighed it. And they always charged us for the abrasion loss. When I sent those two-and-a-half-dollar gold pieces over there (worth a small fortune in 1933 and worth a lot more today), I called up and said, 'We're sending the gold pieces over, but I want to ask one favor of you.'

" 'All right, what is it?'

" 'This is serious. I mean it. Don't make an abrasion on them. If you do, you're going to have one of the most ardent haters of the Federal Government that ever was – me. And I'll never get over it. You take those coins that have a collector's value and you melt them down. That's a crime in itself; but it would be a worse crime to make us turn them in and pay an abrasion charge too.'

" 'I don't know what I can do, but I'll see.'

" 'Well, it's serious and you'd better take it up with Dallas before you send us any charge on this.'

"We never heard any more from it, so they decided it was worth paying attention to."[3]

Only a part of the reforming energy of the New Deal expended itself in remodeling and regulating our financial institutions. The rest flowed into an ever-expanding effort to feed the hungry and find work for the jobless. The Federal Emergency Relief Administration was passing government money on to state and local relief agencies within three months of the inauguration. As late as January 1, 1933, the El Paso *Times* could say, "Under our political economy . . . the people support the government; the government does not support the people," but our leaders learned as quickly as other Americans to hold out their hands for government money. Mayor Ray Sherman expressed the new point of view on June 30, 1933: "We have found that people have to be fed whether they work or not. We have learned that children have to be educated and their lives protected though the parents' earning power be nil. . . . It has taken this great depression to teach us that prosperity must begin at the bottom — with the masses."[4]

President Roosevelt said it another way in his inaugural address: "It is the inherent duty of the Federal Government to keep its citizens from starving."

The administration, it must be admitted, believed that it was better for a man to earn his bread than to take it as a gift, and the alphabet agencies began offering jobs to all who had not discovered that being on relief was a satisfactory way of life. The Civil Works Administration arrived in El Paso on November 4, 1933, and set up projects which gave employment to 4,000 men with another 4,000 signed up waiting to be called.[5] The CWA was succeeded by the Public Works Administartion as pump-priming went into high gear. Many projects in El Paso were paid for by money allocated for PWA use. Streets were opened, prime examples being Brown Street and Alabama Avenue. Records were sorted and catalogued. Newspaper files in the library were indexed. The Rio Grande was straightened and channeled under a River Rectification Program. The College of Mines saw more blasting and building on its rocky campus than in all its previous history as ground was leveled, walls were erected, and buildings were built. Paving for the Scenic Drive, long overdue, was finally put down with the help of government money.[6] The PWA, the RFC, the TRC, and all the other multiplying agencies ran the national debt up to heights undreamed of by the founding fathers, but they provided the bridge over which we passed to better times.

Anything which brought business closer to normal was naturally good for the El Paso banks. They were directly benefited when borrowing from local banks was authorized by the FHA for building projects and business enterprises. At the very end of 1934 the Board of Directors of the State National authorized bank officers to "make application to the Federal Housing Administration for approval as mortgagee under the provision of Title II of the National Housing Act; to submit applications to the Federal Housing Administration for mortgages under Title II; and to enter into any agreements, execute any documents or papers, and furnish any information required or deemed necessary or proper by the Federal Housing Administration in effecting such application and such insurance."[7]

Through the worst days the bank had kept its head well above water. Deposits had declined in 1931, 1932 and 1933 as much as a million and a half dollars below the pre-1929 normal, but this was nothing to be very much alarmed about, and by 1934 deposits were above the 1929 level.[8]

In 1931 Bassett and Flory had watched the downswing with concern if not with alarm. Flory wanted to leave his money to the Bassett girls and talked to his partner about it. Bassett said, "Leave it to me. I'll see that they get it when the time comes. In the meantime, I might need it."[9]

There was never any doubt that the bank would survive, and business steadily improved as El Paso emerged gradually from the Depression. Confidence came back with tougher banking regulations. More cash went into circulation as more soldiers and bigger payrolls came to Fort Bliss. Ten million men were still unemployed at the end of 1935, but the *Times* for December 15 announced that the amount of money going into new automobiles was up 40 percent. Home construction was on the rise. The *Herald-Post* on January 1, 1937, editorialized cheerfully: "Economically we are on the upward road. . . . Socially we have made notable progress toward greater security for wage earners, the dependent and the aged." In 1930 the population of El Paso was 102,241. In 1940 it was 98,801. The decline showed how hard the struggle had been. But in 1939 the great military machine of the Axis began to move on three continents and the last traces of the Depression disappeared as the economy went into high gear.

The war years brought plenty of business but problems of another nature came with the boom. One was the declining health of Mr. Bassett, who had been suffering from hypertension for some time. He had been a very active man all his life and at the age of sixty he began to feel the strain.

The depression years had been difficult for him. His holdings were large – real estate in El Paso, Oklahoma City and California, two lumber yards, a hotel chain with five units in West Texas towns, the Texas Grand Theatre, a New Mexico oil company, a West Texas ranch and shares in a great number of miscellaneous enterprises.[10] Shortly after the crash of 1929, he began construction of the O. T. Bassett Tower, one of our first skyscraper office buildings, on the block where the Bassett Lumber Yard had first opened for business. Through the thirties he scrambled to pay off the indebtedness on it. On June 1, 1934, for instance, he notified the directors, as he was required to do, that he had borrowed $35,000 from the South Texas Commercial Bank of Houston and $75,000 from the First National Bank of Dallas. "The purpose of both these loans is to pay expenses and indebtedness on the O. T. Basset Tower."[11]

At first he moved people into the building at little or no rent so it would not be empty. When his daughter Myra asked him why he started an enterprise as big as that in the middle of such hard times, he replied, "I often wonder."

Driving back from California one time, he said to Hal Daugherty, "You know, Hal, with all my real estate and other holdings, I ought to be a rich man, but I am barely making a living."[12]

He wanted to send his daughters to Europe to learn French and Spanish, but Myra was the only one who actually went, and her education was paid for out of his State National Bank salary. Nothing else was producing any ready money.

Most of these stresses and strains were over by 1940, but when the war clouds began to gather, Mr. Bassett took on extra responsibilities and continued to wear himself out. In 1941 he became regional chairman for the Victory Fund Committee, in charge of raising the first and second War Loans in thirty-two West Texas and New Mexico counties. When the Victory Fund was succeeded by the War Finance Committee, Bassett and Sam Young of the El Paso National alternated as chairman. He was general chairman of four War Bond drives and in each case reached his quota.

Bassett was continuously occupied by civic as well as national duties. He was at one time or another president of the Chamber of Commerce, director of the Community Chest, and president of the Gateway Club. He drew up the Budget System for the City of El Paso.[13] No worth-while civic enterprise during his active years ever asked in vain for his time, advice and constructive effort.

A quiet man who liked to stay in the background, he nevertheless possessed great firmness of character and ran his bank with a sure and decisive touch. There was never any question as to who was in charge. If every officer in the bank favored making a particular loan and Mr. Bassett opposed it, the loan was not made.[14]

He was admired, respected, and even feared by his employees, but a quiet sense of humor saved him from becoming a terrifying presence in the bank. It gave young Hal Daugherty the courage to approach him in 1938 to suggest that he and Myra, the eldest Bassett daughter, wanted to get married. Hal had been with the bank since 1923 and had known Myra since she was a young girl dashing in to keep a luncheon date with George Flory. He had come to know her better when she worked for a short time at the bank. Now the affair was at the point where her father had to be consulted. Myra broached the subject to him. Mr. Bassett immediately remembered that his own mother and other members of the family had died of "consumption." "Well," he said, "at least he's too old to get tuberculosis."

When he proved reluctant to let Myra marry anybody, Hal approached him. "You know all about me, Mr. Bassett. What am I supposed to say when I ask Myra's hand in marriage? I don't know very much about this."

"Well, son, I haven't done it before myself."

"I guess I am supposed to talk about my future. Hell, you know a lot more about my future than I do."

Mr. Bassett had to laugh, and made no further opposition.[15]

In 1943 he was forced to give up active management of the bank. High blood pressure and internal bleeding warned him that his health was failing and he went to Santa Monica, California, where he had business interests and a summer home.[16] In December he asked to be relieved of his duties as president of the bank and the directors offered him the chairmanship of the board. At the annual meeting on January 11, 1944, Maury Kemp (attorney for the bank and long-time board member) read Mr. Bassett's letter of acceptance:

> I have been at the helm a long time. I feel I am entitled to be free of the hard work and many responsibilities incident to the presidency of the bank. I am therefore accepting the newly created office of 'Chairman of the Board of Directors.' In this capacity I shall continue to keep in close contact with the bank, its policy and progress; as would be natural in view of my stock ownership and my deep personal interest in the institution. My successor, from long years of service with the bank, is thoroughly familiar with its plans and its policies, which he helped to inaugurate and develop, and the same is true of his followers, in succession, who have grown up with the bank.

Five months later he died in a Santa Monica hospital and El Paso mourned his passing. "This community has lost one of the best citizens it ever had," said Mayor Anderson in the *Herald-Post* for June 10. "He was one of El Paso's most substantial citizens and one of its builders."

The most fitting tribute was spread on the minutes of the board of directors:

> During all the intervening years between his selection as president and his retirement as Chairman of the Board, he gave the best of his physical, mental and spiritual efforts to the upbuilding and maintaining of (and we say it with righteous pride) the best bank in the great South-

west. The growth and stability of our bank is the best evidence of his ability, courage and faithfulness to his obligations. . . . Be it resolved by the Board of Directors of The State National Bank of El Paso that the Bank has lost a great executive and a great leader. We individually have lost a true and loyal friend and supporter. He was a big tree in the forest of men, and when he fell, there was a wide clearing.[17]

Calm, reasonable Robert W. McAfee was the new president, an employee since 1917, when he had left his job as bookkeeper for the Bassett Lumber Yard to fill a vacancy at the bank. With a first-class board of directors, including such fine personalities and businessmen as H. L. Birney, Gus Momsen, B. F. Darbyshire, Dexter Mapel and Maury Kemp, and such officers as George Matkin, Walter Scott, Hal Daugherty, Forrest Smith, Paul Anderson, Guyler Magruder, Al Uhlig, Bill Hanley, and Bert Neugebauer, the bank was in good hands. The great war was in full swing, however, and it brought new problems to the management.

For one thing, every able-bodied young man went off to serve his country and the personnel situation became a nightmare. The turnover exceeded 100% for some time. Later on when the Korean trouble broke out, a good many of the young men were recalled and the nightmare was repeated. As the number of male employees decreased, a greater percentage of women were hired, and it was surprising how many of them were Principal Clyde Wafer's ex-students from Ysleta High School. Army wives, college girls, high-school graduates, girls who had taken business courses — they came in from everywhere. And they moved on much too fast to suit the officers of the bank. The permanent employees had to keep at the everlasting task of training the new acquisitions, and it was always an uphill battle. "We just threw them in there," says Bill Hanley of those difficult days, "and sweated it out. We had some fine ones and we had some sorry ones. And some of the good ones are still here."

"We all had to pitch in," Bill continues. "Many times Forrest Smith and I would relieve cages while the men went to lunch. Forrest was a vice president but that didn't matter. The work was there and it had to be done.

"We started hiring girl bookkeepers at that time. The first one was Marian Billingsley. She is married to Vice President Freeman

Harris. Frances Arledge, who is now one of our two women officers, started as a bookkeeper. She came in as a student worker – part time – and worked during a summer. She completed her education, became a CPA, and is still with us. She was a high-school kid when I hired her."[18]

By the beginning of the year 1945, hope began to rise that the war would soon be over. The allies were getting the upper hand on all fronts and people realized that the problems of peace might well be as pressing as the problems of war. Short rations, shortages in housing, and insufficiencies in all kinds of consumer goods had been the rule for four years. Even with production going at full blast, it would take a long time to catch up. Housing was the great need. "Defense homes" – minimum-cost units – were available for a favored few, but plumbers and electricians and carpenters were all in the army, building materials were hard to find, and the delays in getting anything done were heartbreaking. Old houses could be repaired at a cost of no more than $200 per year, but it was so difficult to get applications through the WPB and the FHA that only a courageous man would try it. All this created a mighty backlog of business which would mean intense activity for builders and bankers the minute peace became a reality.

On August 6 the bomb fell on Hiroshima. Four days later El Paso was well along in planning for the V-J Day celebration. Colonel John E. Blaine, Security and Intelligence Officer at Fort Bliss, said he would send a detachment of a hundred military policemen to keep order in the downtown area. Bars would be closed for forty-eight hours. Churches would be open for those who wished to pray. There would be a victory rally in El Paso High School stadium.

News of the surrender came on August 14 and that night was given over to joy and thanksgiving. It was not all hilarity. Women knelt in the streets to thank the Lord for stopping the killing. In the hearts of those who jammed San Jacinto Plaza that evening, there was relief and gratitude far deeper than they could express in a noisy celebration. The next day the end of gas rationing was announced, and the ordeal was over.[19]

At The State National Bank the officers were already getting set for the coming boom. Jobs were waiting for the men who had been away. Two would not come back: William Chappell and C. G. Barlow, killed in action. On January 9, 1945, their sacrifice was commemorated at the annual meeting. All the rest had come through safely, and their services were badly needed.

Short handed and short tempered as the bank officials were during the war years, the last thing they could complain of was lack of business. Their real problem was keeping up with what they had. The explosive growth of Fort Bliss and the expansion of the missile ranges northward from El Paso in the Tularosa Basin brought steady streams of revenue to banks and business houses. RFC loans to irrigation projects, small businesses, factories, and builders brought more. In 1935 the State National, in desperate need of more working space, had found it necessary to rent the adjoining building on the west (the China Palace), install doorways, and move into the lower floor. In 1941 the directors bought the building from Mrs. Ida Pfaff. In the same year they began work on a new annex to replace Mrs. Pfaff's building and completed it in January, 1942 – two stories and a basement, all air conditioned. Six years later – in 1948 – it all had to be done over again. This time the bank expanded to the south or rear. A second annex provided such necessities as quarters for the senior officers, a board room, and (in the basement) a coffee room and a bigger mail room.[20]

The annual statements of condition show what was going on. Assets were listed as follows:

June 30, 1931	$13,441,605.54
June 30, 1941	27,342,399.93
June 30, 1951	80,429,472.93
March 31, 1952	95,591,256.04

The fact that money was flowing freely was reflected in the interest rates paid on deposits. In 1934 the rate was 2½% on sums up to $10,000. In 1935 it was 2% up to $5,000. In 1941 it went down to 1%.[21]

Another index of prosperity was a steady increase in capitalization. After the expansion of 1920, when Mr. Morehead was forced out of the saddle, capitalization held steady at $300,000 until 1945. In that year it was doubled. In 1948 it was doubled again. In 1950 a 25% stock dividend raised it to $1,500,000.[22]

Boom times for El Paso began in 1945 and the prosperity of the bank was part of the general forward movement. For the next twenty years, however, imagination, foresight, and a genuine concern for the welfare of the community played their parts in shaping the future of The State National Bank of El Paso. The result was an era of expansion and development of which Mr. Morehead and Mr. Magoffin in 1881 could never have dreamed.

BACK TO PROSPERITY

• PROSPERITY IS A FINE THING to have, but it doesn't come cheap. For The State National Bank of El Paso, the quarter century since Hitler's war machine collapsed has been a time of rapid growth and steady expansion of services. It would be a bad mistake, however, to suppose that all this progress and prosperity was achieved without blood, sweat, and a few tears. For a banker, there is never any such thing as security, though securities are part of his business. He is a driver on a narrow mountain road with disaster at his elbow. He is a ship's captain navigating in rough and dangerous waters where sharks are waiting, and if he wrecks his ship, they pick his bones without listening to his explanations. The history of the bank during the last twenty-five years is a success story, but the success was not automatic. Behind it was shrewd planning, receptiveness to new ideas, and a tremendous amount of hard work on the part of George Matkin, Hal Daugherty, Walter Scott, and the entire crew of the State National.

Better times began the moment the shooting stopped. El Paso had a lot of catching up to do, however, and there was a period of readjustment as the economy reorganized and business leaders got their feet on the ground. By 1948 the post-war boom was on. The value of new construction for the year 1950 was $25,000,000.[1] With some ups and downs it has risen steadily ever since. In 1966 it was $59,000,000.[2] El Paso, a growing town at the end of the war, exploded into big-city status, bursting its seams as it expanded in all directions. New subdivisions mushroomed on the slopes of Mount Franklin, on the Alamogordo and Carlsbad highways, in the Upper and Lower Valleys. Everywhere you looked, there was a new commercial district or shopping center. The city limits were moved beyond the Country Club on the north and as far south as Ysleta in order to bring some sort of order and regulation to the fantastic growth of the suburbs. One year the purple verbenas carpeted the sandhills in the spring. The next, malls and parking lots had sprouted in their place.

The population grew at ten times the national average. In 1940, 96,801 people called El Paso home. In 1950 there were 130,385. Between 1957 and 1967 the figures doubled, reaching 330,000. El Paso was the fastest-growing city in Texas, and Juarez, across the river, grew even faster. The two communities in 1971 number over three-quarters of a million, and before we know it, the million mark will have been passed.

Money poured into the construction of new housing, new school buildings, new streets and highways, and at the same time a series of big construction projects kept employment high and the supply services busy: Paisano Drive (1947); the Bataan Memorial Trainway (1950); the cross-town freeway (1969) and the north-south freeway, (not yet completed); the relocation of the Rio Grande and building activities along the international boundary after the Chamizal settlement of 1967, activities which will be in progress for some time.

The United States Government was heavily involved in almost every aspect of the boom, authorizing loans for light and heavy construction, helping to finance the freeways, paying off service men and civilians at Fort Bliss to the tune of many millions of dollars a year. The payroll in 1950 was $13,500,000. In 1967 it was $120,000,000, while Fort Bliss and the missile ranges contributed an additional estimated sixty million to the El Paso economy in contracts and purchases.[3]

All this activity naturally was good for the banking business. In 1950 four banks were operating within the city limits, and all of them, including the State National, took full advantage of the upswing. As a result, SNB assets of eighty million dollars in 1951 had grown to 184 million in 1970.[4]

Loans and savings, trust accounts and bond transactions – all the normal activities of a bank – built profits, but the management did not just sit back and watch income and resources multiply. It undertook one huge development program on its own. This was the Charles N. Bassett Center, opened in 1963, one of the largest and finest shopping centers anywhere.

The Bassett family and The State National Bank owned jointly several parcels of land in El Paso, among them the Ascarate tract which was acquired through foreclosure away back in 1898. Part of it lay between Montana Avenue and the route of the cross-town freeway in East El Paso, an area which was bound to boom eventually, but which for many years brought in no revenue except from a sand pit which operated in the exact middle of the future shopping center. When the time seemed ripe, bank officials and family representatives decided to start building. "Some promoters came along and told us how easy it was," Hal Daugherty says, "and for five years it damn near killed George Matkin and me. But we didn't want somebody fifty years from now to say, 'You know we once owned all this but those dumb old meatheads sold it all off.' "[5]

Those five years, 1958 to 1963, were really strenuous for the planners and financers. One difficulty was the mass of local, state and national regulations which got in each other's way and made it hard for a developer to stay within the law. As a way of making sure everything was legal, the bank organized a subsidiary corporation, the Flory Company, which could hold property and enter business relations when the bank could not. It was created in 1959 and soon had assets of over half a million dollars, including Bassett Center stock and debentures.[6]

Bassett Center, when it was completed, occupied fifty-six acres of land and cost over seven million dollars. The corporation formed to build it is now headed by Hal Daugherty, Vice-Chairman of the Board of Directors of the State National, with George Matkin, Chairman of the Board, as first vice-president.[7] The Bassett National Bank, doing business at the center, has working connections as well as sentimental ties, with the State National. The new bank uses the SNB computer system for processing its own accounts.

It would be easy to multiply examples of ways in which the bank increased its business. Cotton loans would be one. Big cotton buyers borrowed as much as seventeen millions of dollars in short-term loans when the crop was coming in.[8] The bank participated also in mortgage loans negotiated to carry on government housing projects — like the Abilene Air Force Base in 1957, the Holloman Air Force Base in 1958.[9] New industries, attracted by our fine climate and unlimited labor force, built factories which made everything from spurs and saddles to telescopic sights and Mexican food. Between 1963 and 1967 eighty new firms opened their doors in our community.[10] A surprising number of them were clothing manufacturers – so many, in fact, that El Paso now claims to be the largest center in the world for the manufacture of men's and boys' slacks, maintaining a labor force of nearly 20,000 people.[11] In every area of expansion The State National Bank stood ready to furnish financial sinew to reliable and competent men, and so many of them applied for loans that through the Fifties the bank had to screen their applications with the utmost care, accepting only the best accounts. The amount of money available for loans is limited by law – ten percent of capital and surplus – and the only way a bank can increase its lending capacity is to build up its reserves.

In his annual message to the stockholders on January 8, 1951, President George Matkin discussed the situation. "The demand for loans has been terrific. In March of this year [1950] the Voluntary Credit Control Program was initiated. The purpose of Voluntary Credit Control, as stated, was to try to hold the inflation down by making money tighter. It was given to the banks on a voluntary basis, but with enough publicity, and enough talk, to where the banks of this country felt that they had their choice of living up to this control program or seeing legislation put on the statue books which would make the voluntary program compulsory."

With so much activity the bank naturally made money. Deposits increased by over eleven million dollars in 1951 – to ninety-six and a half million. Assets for the first time in history went over $100,000,000.

Could any banker ask for anything more? This was success with a capital S, the banker's dream fulfilled, happiness, security, joy.

Well, not quite all that! There were plenty of headaches.

There was always the weather to worry about. Cotton and cattle have to have moisture. When the water behind Elephant Butte Dam is low, the cotton farmers face disaster, and when there is not enough rainfall to sprout grass and weeds, cattlemen look grim and try to get the bank to extend their notes. Never be surprised if you see a banker watching the sky. He has reason enough.

The early fifties were dry years. George Matkin, closing his report for 1951, faced the future "with apprehension as to the farming situation in our valley, due to insufficient water in Elephant Butte Dam, to make the next crop, and with the hope and prayer that World Peace and the drought conditions will both be clarified before the closing of another year." It was the banker's yearly petition: "Lord, give us peace and precipitation!"

The late fifties were better as far as water was concerned, but business throughout the country declined. Matkin reported on January 13, 1959, "In 1958 the country was in a depression." Locally, he added, "we did not feel this except in a few cases. . . . El Paso had a banner year in building, with the largest number of building permits in our history. The farmer and cattleman made a comeback, and at the close of the year bank deposits were the biggest ever published for the city of El Paso."

Again in 1961 the country was in "a serious recession." This time El Paso really felt it. Building was off. Department-store sales were down. Bank clearings dropped. The cotton farmers came out ahead, but "the cattle people did not fare as well, with little moisture and lower prices."[12]

A worry even more pressing than the rainfall and business cycles was taxes. Matkin pointed out in his 1951 report that State and county taxes amounted to $86,000 – a sum which he considered "rather staggering." He estimated that the income tax would be $465,000 – even more staggering. As the years went by, taxes increased for the bank, as they did for all other individuals and institutions. In 1967 the bank's outlay for taxes was over a million dollars. A word stronger than "staggering" would have to be found to comment adequately on this situation.

Next to taxes probably the biggest headache for the management of the State National has been people – officers and employees. The turnover through the fifties and into the sixties was appalling. "The disturbing thing about our employee problems," Matkin reported in 1951, "is that banks have always used young men for many of their positions, and most of the young men are being drafted or going back into the armed services. During the year we hired 161 employees and lost 151."

It got worse before it got better. "In 1955 a total of 206 employees were hired and 202 were lost. . . . We find more clerical help seeking work with companies that work only five days a week, and we find more clerical help that are expecting more pay than banks have been giving. As a result of this, we have changed our pay scale to some extent, and think that it will be more acceptable in the coming year."[13] In 1967 the situation was much improved but still not ideal. The staff totaled 344, and of these 159 terminated employment and had to be replaced.

Hardest to lose were the faithful ones who had given many years of loyal service to the bank – such stalwarts as Lawrence "Sag" Shea, Constance Pateman, Evie Wimberly, Irene Schwankhaus. Death claimed others. Paul Anderson (1949) and Dudley Wallen (1967) were officers widely known, respected and beloved in the community. An especially tragic happening in 1961 was the death by asphyxiation of Al Uhlig and his wife Julia as a result of a fire in their home. Two very attractive and likable people, they met in the bank when Julia was a clerical employee and Al was a junior officer, and they had spent their mature lives under the wing of SNB. In 1963 R. W. McAfee, Jr., only son of the Honorary Chairman of the Board, died after an extended illness, thereby hastening the demise of his father.

The senior McAfee came to El Paso from Indiana in 1907 at the invitation of C. N. Bassett, who had been his roommate in college days. He managed the Bassett Lumber Company until he was called to the bank as Cashier in 1917. He became President on Mr. Bassett's death in 1944 and Chairman of the Board in 1949. His health began to fail in the 1950's at a time when aggressive leadership was needed. In 1960 he became Honorary Chairman of the Board with no formal responsibilities in the bank, but he maintained an office and came to work every day. His mental functions became so impaired, however, that he could not find his way back to his office when he left it to visit the bank lobby. Mr. McAfee was much beloved by his fellow officers and they gave him all the care and help they could, but the day came when he had to give up and go home for good. He did not want to leave. It broke his heart to think of it. When he finally made his last exit, he got half way across Oregon Street; then stopped and stood still with traffic swirling around him. Guyler Magruder saw him there, crying, and hurried to his side. "Mr. McAfee," he said, "you can't stand here. You might get killed."

"I don't care," he replied. But he got into the taxi Magruder called, making no protest, and went away. When he died on April 22, 1967, the bank lost a man who, in his day, had been one of its pillars. Jack Clark still carries in his wallet the little note Mr. McAfee wrote him when he retired, and in many another heart his memory is cherished.[14]

In a very few cases good men were lost to the bank because of greater opportunities elsewhere. Forrest Smith, a tower of strength in the cashier's position, resigned in 1952 to become president of a bank in San Antonio. Edward Arnold accepted the presidency of the Bassett National Bank in 1966. William Emig was lured away to Albuquerque in 1967.

These are rare occurrences. Most of the officers have stayed with the ship and waited for promotion. Sometimes it took ten, fifteen, twenty years for a vacancy to occur, but when it came, the replacement, trained and seasoned, was ready to fill the vacant chair. Mr. Bassett's final message to the directors has applied through the years: "My successor, from long years of service with the bank, is thoroughly familiar with its plan and its policies, which he helped to inaugurate and develop, and the same is true of his followers, in succession, who have grown up with the bank."

George Matkin was elevated to the presidency in 1949 when R. W. McAfee became Chairman of the Board. Matkin was and is a man of great energy and active mind. He is one of the best-read men the bank has ever had in economic and banking matters – a real asset when keeping up with state and government directives is almost a full-time job. At the same time he has kept the common touch – can communicate on friendly terms with any employee or officer. As president he kept a firm hand on the controls and demanded the best performance his men could give. Everyone in the bank spoke of him with affection and regarded him as a friend. The whole staff was pleased when he became Chairman of the Board in 1967.

The same qualities of democratic friendliness and good-humored dignity characterize H. M. Daugherty, now Vice-Chairman of the Board. Hal thinks of himself as an idea man, always pushing for improvements and constructive changes. He is the link between the Bassett family and the bank and takes the lead where Bassett properties and holdings are involved. Like all men who are good at what they do, he enjoys his job and radiates good feeling and confidence.

Matkin's replacement in the presidency in 1967 was Robert F. Lockhart, at forty-two the youngest man ever to take the helm. Like Matkin, Daugherty and most of the officers, he "grew up with the bank" and learned the business by doing it. He had great energy, drive and concentration. The events which terminated his career as a banker in 1969 constitute the most tragic chapter in the State National's history.

Until the Lockhart bombshell burst, the bank held to the principle that as long as it trained its own officers, there would be steadiness and continuity in the management. Those who passed on would always be mourned, but they would be replaced by men they themselves had educated for the jobs they had to do. The Lockhart case triggered what amounted to a revolution in the hiring and training practices of the State National – a revolution which will be working itself out for a long time to come.

In other ways besides recruiting, the bank has respected tradition and followed conventional practices. To keep the bank prosperous and to stay ahead of the game as much as possible, the management has steered a course between the old ways and the new, with emphasis on caution and care.

For many years, for instance, the officers followed a rule of thumb that funds should be divided about equally – one third in loans, one third in government bonds, one third in cash. Loans have gradually absorbed a greater percentage and will run closer to fifty percent now. Another rule, perhaps not so universally accepted but always observed by the State National, teaches that it is better to build the bank's assets than to pay munificent dividends. The policy of the State National under Matkin's leadership has been to declare adequate dividends but not build them up too high. After all, the stockholders have to pay income tax on these dividends though the bank has already paid on the same money. It seems better for everybody to let surplus and undivided profits grow until it is time for a stock division. A hundred-percent stock dividend was declared in 1955 and again in 1967. The bank's capitalization is now $6,000,000. The stockholders seem to like this way of handling the business.[15]

In many other ways the bank has tried to stay on its toes and improve its business and services without waiting until necessity stepped in and forced the issue. In 1950 ambition to do a better job led to the appointment of Chris P. Fox, ex-sheriff, former manager of the Chamber of Commerce, friend of practically every man, woman and child in El Paso, as the organization's first director of public relations. A serious contender for the world's championship as a long-distance, high-powered rapid-fire speaker, Chris was a natural for his job. Matkin noted in his January, 1951, report the "large volume of mail" going out of Fox's office and he continued to marvel in later reports at the man's ability to make as many speeches a day as were required of him, at the same time keeping up with his work at the bank. Since the start of the Korean involvement, he has turned out a weekly newspaper, the *Home Town News,* for El Pasoans in the armed forces. Typical items from 1970:

Thirty churches will hold a city-wide youth rally at Irvin High, with Rev. Barry Wood of Beverly Hills, Calif., being the pumper-upper. . . . They will close the monkey laboratory at Holloman AFB about January, '71. Wanna monkey? **The new Chancellor at the U. of T., Charles A. Le Maistre, the first thing out of the barn, fired Dr. John R. Silber as Dean of the College of Arts & Sciences at UT. . . . This will bring on much yap-yap. **This is a good way to do it. . . . Henry Roman, 1300 Howze Ave., at 4th and So. El Paso St. saw Mrs. Maria Savary of 805 N. El Paso being mugged, losing her purse, and Henry took out and ran the character down. . . . **Members of our Third Bn. 133rd Arty. TNG are on their way to Ft. Hood for summer training.

The folks in the Ranchland Hills, Lomaland, Mesa Verde and Hacienda Heights areas want City Hall to set up a program to head off more juvenile troubles in that area . . . a Rev. Thomas Parra, the spokesman, said he felt that City Hall was not doing enough to combat delinquency and narcotic troubles in that area. Well, I would say that City Hall is doing the best it can to take care of all that business . . . everywhere . . . and as to the narcotics, they're not going to do any good with that until we ask our friends in Juarez to bring this deluge-flow of narcotics from there into El Paso to a grinding halt. . . . I am sure that, if they are called upon they will respond. **We had the biggest flood and heaviest rain of the season, with rocks and sand and stuff over town, and many flooded basements . . . our area got an inch!

With good efforts by the city, the heavy storm debris is about cleaned up. **El Paso bankers went before the City Brd. of Equalization, which is set up to hear appeals from taxpayers who feel their taxes were too high or were not equal, or something . . . the Times says . . . the Brd. Members were surprised to hear at least one banker say the downtown property evaluation was not high enough . . . that banker was Mr. B. Glen Jordan, President of The State National Bank . . . my bank![16]

Besides putting out the *Home Town News,* Chris has at one time or another produced a daily early-morning radio news commentary, served on the Armed Forces Committee of the Chamber of Commerce, represented the Secretary of the Army as Civilian Aide on armed-forces business, entertained celebrities, and functioned as a celebrity himself.

Year by year improvements and constructive changes have been made. In 1951 the parking lot was expanded (5,103 customers used it in the month of December). In that year a sidewalk teller was in operation. Two Christmas Savings Club were organized. In 1952 Eliot Hermann was employed to install a modern Credit Department, and the Employees' Profit Sharing Fund was created. The bank contributes up to three percent of its earnings before taxes to this fund.

In 1954 the Motorbank went into operation in remodeled quarters across Oregon Street from the main building and a new Auditing Department was created with Roland Scott in charge.

In 1957 the floors above the Motorbank were rebuilt and the new offices were occupied by the Trust Department and the bookkeepers.

For several years after that the big push was towards automation and computerization. A small beginning was made in 1958 and 1959 with the purchase of Addressograph equipment for the Bookkeeping and Trust Departments. By 1960 the management was about ready to computerize the bookkeeping operations of the bank and began to investigate the possibilities and problems — computer types available; difficulties of changing over from a manual system; necessary alterations in the physical facilities; the need for educating the customers.

The first big step was taken on July 7, 1961, when an order was placed with IBM for a "1401 Tape-Oriented System" – in the judgment of the officers the best on the market at that time. While they waited for delivery, the officials made a start toward changing the banking habits of their depositors. On October 6, 1961, all checking accounts were numbered and the bank moved toward the use of numbered checks and deposit tickets.

It took some time to complete the preparations, but the new equipment was finally installed on April 17, 1963. Exactly one month later, on May 17, the first posting of demand deposits was made, and The State National Bank became the first in its area to computerize its bookkeeping and accounting functions.

Service in other areas of banking activity were improved likewise. A xerox machine was acquired in 1965 and a year later an Accounts Receivable service was instituted for doctors and dentists. By 1966 the Trust Department had switched to an electronic Data Processing System. In that year also a "Time of Day" service was introduced which received the unheard-of number of 30,000 calls per day. In 1967 the Installment Loan Department went on the computer.

All this mechanization sometimes caused the old employees to shake their heads and think back to earlier times when banking methods were more primitive. They remembered the days fifty years before when there was a large Chinese colony in El Paso with headquarters on South Oregon Street. Some of the patriarchs had substantial accounts and their business was valued, but their calculating methods were strictly traditional. To accommodate them the bank kept an abacus – the original Chinese computer – on each of the two check desks, and often drew drafts for them in Hong Kong dollars on Hong Kong banks. A postcard arrived every day from a San Francisco house to keep the State National up to date on the value of Chinese money. It was typical of those horse-and-abacus times that the bank supplied Chinese calendars, purchased in San Francisco, to its Oriental customers.[17]

In the long run, of course, the Chinese connections were not of major importance. The big producer of foreign business is and always has been the Mexican Department, and the bank has always striven to improve and enlarge it. R. W. McAfee, Jr., was in charge until his death in 1963. His place was taken by Joe Herrera, formerly city clerk, a man of wide acquaintance among both Anglos and Mexicans on both sides of the border.

"When I started in," Joe says, "I knew absolutely nothing about banking. I couldn't keep my own checkbook balanced." But Joe caught on, with persistence and help. Hal Daugherty took him to Chihuahua and introduced him to the right people. His new colleagues gladly answered his questions. He visited banks in Mexico and entertained bankers when they came to El Paso. "I learned the hard way," he says. But he learned.[18]

The traffic in Mexican pesos has been an important part of the bank's business for some time. The total number of pesos handled in 1967 was 416,892,670; in 1968 it was 464,279,427; and the following year, 472,260,931. Merchants deposit these pesos or exchange them for dollars, and the bank sells them to banks in Juarez. Since armed guards from the United States are not allowed in Mexico, the Juarez banks send messengers every morning to pick up the money.[19]

As important as any division in the bank, and one in which it takes special pride, is the Trust Department. From small beginnings back in 1920, it has come a long way. In 1970 its assets were over $87,000,000.[20] The working force consists of over thirty people, of whom eleven are officers. A full-time administrator and supervisor, with the title of Assistant Trust Officer, is needed to take care of the farm and ranch property entrusted to the bank. The State National Bank Foundation is handled by the Trust Department, as are the bank's pension plan and profit-sharing plan. Trust affairs were directed for many years by Walter W. Scott, the senior bank employee in terms of length of service – a man of great experience and wisdom, firm character and extraordinary personal charm. In 1970 Martin Kern stepped in as vice-president and manager of the division.

The State National Bank has indeed prospered during the quarter century since 1945. It has grown tremendously and seems in 1971 on the verge of still more phenomenal developments. There have been bad times and good times, boom years and recessions, losses to balance the gains, but those intervening years have been for the men who lived through them an adventurous and exciting time.

FULL SERVICE

• A few years ago a familiar figure at the State National was Mr. John R. Dalby, who served as a greeter and welcomer to all who entered the bank. Mr. Dalby had been agent for the Texas and Pacific in El Paso and was well known and universally beloved in the community. For years he made a practice of sending a single red rose to each of his friends on his birthday, and he had so many friends that he was practically in the rose business. He was a plain, homespun sort of person, and yet there was a courtliness about him which came from his love of his fellow man and his very real concern for their welfare. He enjoyed being a greeter and welcomer, and every customer to whom he spoke felt as if the entire bank and its services had been turned over to him for as long as he wanted or needed them.

Mr. Dalby, in his special way, was the Spirit of the SNB – a kindly man in a brown suit who made his living by looking out for his neighbor's interests. Today, every officer in the bank has some of his concern for the people who come through the big bronze doors. Everybody, in fact, is trained to combine courtesy with dignity, and the executives pass the lesson on to the young men and women who are placed in their charge. The State National is classified as a Full Service Bank (the Foundation for Commercial Banks awards the title)[1] and has all the services – loan, deposit, trust, safekeeping, savings, – that good banks everywhere are prepared to offer, plus many special ones like the accounts-receivable service for doctors and dentists, the real estate collection service for property owners, and the stock-transfer service – fifty-six of them in all.[2] There is more to service, however, than just the multiplication of departments in the bank. It is something that is given by people to people. In the last analysis, it is a matter of personal helpfulness. The State National, like any well run business, offers good and faithful service to its stockholders, its employees, its customers and its community.

This helpfulness begins at the top. The officers do their utmost, as we have already seen, to give the stockholders the best deal possible. They are also, as Walter Scott puts it, "employee conscious," being mindful and careful about the welfare of the men and women who give their lives to the bank. Mr. Flory in his day masked his concern by assuming a gruff manner, but his grumbling was really constructive. "He used to fuss at people all the time," Sidney Howard remembers. "One time he fussed at me. I went out in the winter time – we used to have to go out and get coffee; we didn't have a coffee room – and I dashed out in my shirt sleeves. He raised the devil with me when I came back. He said, by gosh, they were paying me to work and not get sick around here. If I was going to go out, I could put my coat on. He rode herd on everybody."[3]

Back in 1923, when Evie Wimberly joined the bookkeeping department, the girls had a small lounge where they went to put on their lipstick, if and when they felt the urge. "You just worked," she says. "You didn't care how you looked, really." They did eat their lunches there, and when more people were hired and the place got crowded, they asked Forrest Smith (cashier and personnel officer), "Can't we have a better place to eat our lunches?" He agreed, fixed up a counter in another room and brought in a cooler for cokes.

"They put a little savings bank down there," Evie recalls, "And there was a little hand pointing down with a sign underneath: 'Deposit Coin Here. Honor System.' It wasn't very long until the cokes were all removed. I said, 'Forrest, what happened to the cokes?' And he said, 'The honor system went broke.' Later Mr. Daugherty saw to it that we had a nice coffee shop. He has done a lot of work on it. And he put in two hospital rooms. The first one was back of Safe Deposit and the other is over in the Motorbank building. Mr. Daugherty always saw to it that we had the best equipment the bank would allow him to buy."[4]

The Profit Sharing Plan (1952) and the Retirement Plan (1966) are the result of this same concern for the welfare of the human beings who make their living in the bank. Such services make something alive out of the State National.

In a way the officers have always run a banking school. The policy until 1970 was to bring in ambitious boys and give them a chance to make something of themselves. The first job was runner or mail boy. Runners did errands, in the bank and in town. They worked in the mail room and delivered letters. They pushed "busses," or money carts, around the bank. "When I first came to work," Bert Neugebauer says, "you started out as a runner and you were a runner for some time. Then they put you on a machine to run straight lists to get used to the adding machine. And then you were put on as a sort of assistant bookkeeper from there. And that took months. Then you were a bookkeeper; then you went in as assistant teller; and from there you might go to the collection exchange window or to the paying teller's window. You worked up to number-one paying teller, which meant you were the head teller. You were in charge of the vault – money supply, and so forth. Then you went into the loans and discounts. That used to be the routine, more or less. Not any more. It depends on the individual. At that time we didn't have many college graduates. Now we get more and more of them. A man with a college education, if he wants to apply himself, can do a lot of things that an ordinary high-school graduate can't."[5]

Until recent times, most of the officers followed a routine something like Neugebauer's. Riley Brown, now a commercial loan officer, went to work in 1944 as a coin wrapper. Later he was put into the mail room. "That was a promotion for me,"[6] he says. The day of Al Uhlig's tragic death, Riley was ready to pick up where Al left off.

James Alcorn started in the mail room in 1941 and worked as a messenger. "There was no other way,"[7] he says. R. E. Austin did the same in 1936. One of his jobs was to run down hot checks – take them to the merchants who were the endorsers. "We used to go up through what they called the Proof and Transit Department," he remembers, "approving deposits as they came in. We relieved in the cages as tellers during the noon hour when the boys were out to lunch. We did teller work and ended up in the bookkeeping department, usually, and stayed there for a while. Most of us worked in nearly every department in the bank at one time or another, for short periods. You get the overall comprehensive picture that way."[8]

Ray Adams, now in charge of Savings, came later than these men and did not have to start so near the bottom. He began in 1946 as a bookkeeper. After a year in the books and a year as teller, Ray went into Savings. That, he says, "was quite a jump. I remember when Bill Hanley came in and said, 'You're going to work in the Savings Department.' I said, 'Well, Bill, is this going to be temporary duty?' He said, 'It could be a year, or it could be thirty or forty.' It's been twenty now. So evidently it was a fairly permanent transfer."[9]

The pattern of training for the young men depended more on example than on precept. Not many rules were laid down for them, but they evolved into well mannered, neatly dressed, quietly dignified executives. The fact that there was a shoe-shining machine in the men's rest room on the lobby floor was no doubt one way of telling the boys something. The machine is still there teaching its wordless lesson. The fact that top officers wear clean shirts and keep their hair cut is another object lesson. Crew cuts have largely disappeared and sideburns luxuriate on a young banker's cheek here and there, but the Biblical hair-do for men has not yet invaded the State National.

With or without verbal communication the educational process goes on, and good manners and forbearance on the part of the president and the chairman of the board offer useful lessons to those below them in rank. A story is told about George Matkin that makes the point. Curtis Morris, a particular friend of his, borrowed a large sum of money from the bank to buy a ranch in Mexico. Matkin made the loan. Curtis disappeared south of the border and worked hard, but it took him two years to pay off. Finally he came to Matkin's office, after making the final payment, and got rid of two years of exasperation. "You SOB," he said, "I've paid the last dollar and you know what you can do with the money and the bank and everything else. I'm through with you!" He said it facetiously and with a smile, but he said it.

George answered with perfect courtesy, "Curtis, I am glad you have got through with it and have been able to pay off."

Six months later Curtis was back. He had to refinance for some reason and asked George for another loan. George had not forgotten their last interview. "Well," he said, "it seems to me the last time I saw you, you called me an SOB."

"Of course I did," Curtis replied. That means Safe Old Banker."[10]

Some formal training is made available. Bankers' Institutes are sometimes organized with lectures on matters of professional interest by knowledgeable people. Officers are encouraged to attend conventions, meet their opposite numbers in other banks, and develop a feeling of belonging to something important. When Doris Ryan became an assistant trust officer in 1967 (the first woman to be so honored by the bank), she was asked what convention she would like to attend. She decided to go to the regional meeting of the NAWB(National Association of Women Bankers). "I think I made a good choice," she says.[11] Women bankers are still somewhat rare and need to get together for mutual support.

James Wadley, trust officer, was one who went outside to supplement his education. In the summer of 1962 he completed a three-year Trust course and graduated from the Southwestern School of Banking at Southern Methodist University. A number of boys working in the bank are taking courses at The University of Texas at El Paso and the percentage of college-trained employees is rising steadily.

The old methods produced some good men. One who was grateful for his practical education was E. Edward Arnold, now president of the Bassett National Bank. "I have been with the State National for twenty years," he wrote in his letter of resignation before assuming his new office. "During this time, through classes and graduate courses in banking practices and principles, and exposure in various departments, the State National has made it possible for me to enrich my knowledge to the point where I feel qualified to fill the position at the Bassett National Bank.

"I am deeply indebted to so many people at The State National Bank for so much assistance and encouragement that it is not easy for me to take this action. . . . I shall endeavor to instill, in the Bassett National Bank, the same fine principles which the State National represents to the people of El Paso."

The men and women who have stayed with the SNB over a period of years have done so because they liked what they were doing and appreciated the efforts that were made to help them do it well. They worked long hours, far into the night sometimes, and came to work early when there was catching up to do. And there was never any complaint. One reason was that some of them, at least, knew the joy of service. "I was young, I was ambitious, and I enjoyed people" – Evie Wimberly speaking – "and I felt that I was giving service not only to the bank but to the people. Homes to be built. Education. Children saving their money. One rewarding thing was the way children would come in – children that are grown now – and say, 'Will you help me save my first dollar?'

"Some of those youngsters did strange things. I had many experiences when I was in Savings. I remember that a little boy and his mother came in one day and he gave me his savings bank. It was in terrible shape – all rusty and messy. 'What in the world had happened to it?' I asked the mother. 'Oh,' she said, 'he loves his bank better than anything in the world. He takes it with him when he has his bath.' "[12]

The theory appears to be that if the bank takes good care of its employees, the employees will take good care of the customers, and the system seems to work. It is important that the customers be reminded that the bank wants to and intends to take good care of them. Reminders go out in a variety of forms – newspaper advertisements and friendly little paragraphs tucked in with bank statements, for instance. An especially effective method is the "Officers' Call" system in which all officers participate. Each one is assigned an average of two calls a week. The recipient of the call may be a prospect; he may be a customer already.

"We let them know that we appreciate their business," Riley Brown explains, "but mainly we want to make them aware of services we offer that perhaps they may not be using or may not be aware of – like the fact that a businessman can make treasury tax and loan payments directly to his bank. Of course this is to our advantage as well as his. But people who don't know will just send their money to the Director of Internal Revenue in Austin and the Austin banks profit rather than the El Paso banks."[13]

One service the bank offers as a matter of course is assurance that money on deposit will be safe. This is something customers take for granted. Once the money is in the bank, everybody assumes that it is secure – and it is. But the State National takes no chances. Three or four special officers, including a genial policeman named Tom Brennan, make themselves visible in the lobby during banking hours, but they are not entirely on their own. "They have several concealed cameras taking pictures all the time," Tom says. "Everybody who comes into the bank is photographed without his knowing it. The pictures are very clear and can be compared with police photos for positive identification. Anybody staging a holdup would probably be caught by the camera. The tellers can operate it from where they are standing."[14]

"They take pictures once every thirty seconds," adds Sidney Howard. "And each teller has a button that he can activate and take up to thirty pictures a second. That speeds it up so they make sure they get pictures. There are cameras over each one of the doors and cameras facing the floor from the back of the cages so we get shots from all different angles."

The film will not be processed unless pictures should actually be needed. It will be kept for several months and then destroyed.

The bank is also protected by a burglar alarm which is hooked up with the cages. By stepping on a button, a teller can set off an alarm down at the police station – not heard in the bank. "We still have the clanging bell," Howard says, "but it is wired to the vault in case somebody sets it off at night. It will ring even if the electricity is cut off. It is hooked up to batteries and will ring until the batteries run down. The vaults all have time locks on them anyway, so if the alarm is once set off, it just makes noise the rest of the night."

In spite of all precautions, several attempts have been made to rob the bank. "About three years ago," Sidney Howard says, "a fellow came up to the collection cage over there. I don't really know what he had in mind, and I'm not sure he knew either. He came up to the window and asked for some travelers checks, and while the girl was getting the checks out for him, he pulled out a gun. It scared her so badly that she screamed and ran out of the cage. He fired a couple of shots into the wall over her head and the girl fainted. I don't know whether he was really trying to hit anybody or not. But it shook things up for a while. He got scared himself and ran out to the alley, where he had left his car.

"There happened to be a policeman in the lobby at the time – not a guard; he just happened to be there. When he heard the shot, he ran outside, went around the corner of Oregon and Overland Streets, and caught the man as he was driving out of the alley. The policeman motioned him to stop, and he did. That policeman was braver than I am.

"The man had been in service in Korea – had been wounded and was given a medical discharge. They tried him three times, I think, and I believe they placed him in a mental institution.

"Some time before that a man came up to one of the paying tellers on the other side of the bank and held him up. He got about $2,500, ran out into the alley and got into a taxi. He drove to the side entrance of the Del Norte Hotel – left the taxi waiting outside – and that was the last anybody saw of him. I understand that he wound up across the river in Juarez. The police got a description of him. They even published his name in the paper. But they never caught him. He was an Anglo living in Mexico and is probably still down there. That was seven or eight years ago.

"We had only one other attempted holdup that I know of. A fellow came up to one of the girls with a butcher knife and a sack. He got scared and ran out – didn't get any money."[15]

As a business, the bank's record of service is impressive; as a group of public-spirited citizens the State National has done even better. Every officer of the bank is involved in community affairs ("Off the record, we drive them to it," Hal Daugherty admits),[16] and almost every employee is committed in one way or another to public service. The State National has provided four presidents of the Chamber of Commerce (C. N. Bassett, George Matkin, Hal Daugherty and Chris P. Fox). Every fraternal organization in town owes something to the SNB staff. Boy Scouts (H. H. Edmondson), Girl Scouts (W. M. Updike), the Lighthouse for the Blind (Tom Foster), El Paso Child Welfare Board (Martin Kern), Our Lady's Youth Center (Joe Herrera), Goodwill Industries (W. W. Park), Trans-Pecos Tuberculosis Association (Nathan Cook), Texas Society for Crippled Children (Guyler Magruder), Planned Parenthood of El Paso (Jim Alcorn), National Conference of Christians and Jews (Freeman Harris), Y.M.C.A. (Bob Austin) – all have been supported and officered by bank employees. Half a dozen of the officers work for the United Fund. Jim Alcorn, R. C. McGarr and Donald O'Neill carry the ball for the Rehabilitation Center. Parker Cole and Jim Wadley help in the direction of a school for retarded children. Some of the men carry multiple responsibilities. Bill Purse, for instance is president, vice-president, chairman or director of no less than fifteen civic bodies.

The top men in the bank accept these responsibilities like everybody else. George Matkin, Chairman of the Board, is treasurer of the El Paso Chapter of the Red Cross. Hal Daugherty is treasurer of the El Paso Art Museum. B. Glen Jordan, who became president of the bank in January of 1970, was involved a few months after his appointment as general chairman of business and industrial gifts for the Arthritis Foundation and chairman of the important Agri-Business Committee.

The list could go on and on: Frances Arledge is the secretary-treasurer of the Credit Women's Club. Jim Wadley plays in the El Paso Symphony. Freeman Harris is president of the Community Concert Association. Joe Herrera has just stepped down after a term as president of the El Paso School Board. You name the organization; somebody from the bank will be in it – probably as part of the management.

It is all done cheerfully and gladly, with full realization that good business is a two-way street.

One especially interesting facet of the bank's community service involves the commemoration of historic events and personalities. Always interested in frontier history, which it helped to make, the State National has marked, with bronze plaques, a series of spots where exciting or historic episodes took place: The Pass of the North; San Jacinto Plaza; San Antonio Street, near the Hotel Paso del Norte, where a famous gun battle exploded in 1882; the spot where John Wesley Hardin, most notorious of Texas gunmen, died in 1895. There is no possibility of financial gain from such activities. The officers take pride and pleasure in sponsoring them as a public service – as a gesture of good will to a community in which they and their bank have grown and prospered and in whose development the bank has played such an important role.

THE CASE OF THE MISSING PRESIDENT

• It was easy to like and trust Robert F. Lockhart. A responsible citizen, a model career man, he was living proof of the wisdom and benevolence of the bank's traditional policy: bring in the bright young men early, train them in the way they should go, promote them as far and fast as their efforts and abilities can carry them — even to the very top.

He joined the staff in 1942, just out of Austin High School, and started at the bottom — in the mail room, like everybody else. From the beginning he impressed his co-workers with his diligence and intelligence. Perhaps he was a little over-serious, a little too anxious to do well, a little aloof, a little inclined to drive himself too hard, but these were errors in the right direction. He meant business, and he was going places.

The officers and directors approved of him and brought him along fast. He graduated from the Southwestern School of Banking at Southern Methodist University in 1951 and became an officer in the same year. In 1959 he was made a vice president, and when President George Matkin stepped up to chairman of the board in 1967, Lockhart took over the presidency — the youngest top official in the history of the bank and one of the youngest in the nation. At forty-two he had reached the summit.

Like all officers of the State National, he served his community well. He worked with the Boy Scouts and spent long hours organizing and soliciting for the United Fund. The Chamber of Commerce gave him important committee assignments; the Better Business Bureau made him a director and elected him treasurer; the Goodwill Industries asked him to serve as a director. As a banker he went an extra mile as a director of the El Paso branch of the Federal Reserve Bank of Dallas. As a private citizen he was a faithful member of Unity Christ Church and president of its board. His high school named him its outstanding graduate in October of 1968. He had a fine house in Austin Terrace and two bright, attractive children. Bob Lockhart had it made.

The first indication to the world outside the bank that anything was wrong came in the form of a terse announcement issued to local news media on Friday, March 22, 1969, by Chairman of the Board George Matkin: "Robert F. Lockhart, president of The State National Bank, has resigned his post effective immediately." Matkin added that Lockhart was out of the city and not available for comment.

Two days later the big story hit the front pages. The FBI had been called in. Lockhart had been missing for four days and $60,000 of the bank's money was missing with him. Ray Faisst, special agent in charge of the local FBI office, had filed a complaint with U. S. Commissioner Mario Martinez on Saturday, March 23, the day after Matkin's announcement. He charged that Lockhart had "embezzled, abstracted and purloined the sum of $60,000 in United States currency" from The State National Bank.

By Monday the grapevine had informed every man on the streets of El Paso how it all happened. Lockhart had contrived an elaborate scheme for getting hold of the money. On Tuesday, March 18, the day he disappeared, he instructed clerk Jerry S. Franklin to prepare a shipment of $60,000 for the Van Horn State Bank of Van Horn, Texas. President Clayton McDonald of the out-of-town bank would pick up the cash from a teller at the motor bank. Arthur Olivas, motor bank teller, took charge of the packet and held it.

At 5:30 in the afternoon Olivas got the word that Mr. McDonald would not be able to make the pickup and that President Lockhart would take it himself. Olivas had no reason to question the order. He did as he was instructed and turned over the money when his superior appeared and claimed it. Lockhart walked out with the packet and was seen no more. He did not go home. He just disappeared.

He was actually a desperate man. For over five years he had been living with a dreadful secret. He had made false entries in the bank's records as early as 1964 – long before he became president — and had embezzled in the neighborhood of $25,000. The explanation his lawyers offered later was that he had made bad loans and was ashamed to acknowledge his mistakes. At last there were danger signals. A quiet investigation had begun, and he knew where it would end. Frantic with fear, he prepared to leave before the jaws of the trap closed on him.

In a suitcase he placed some clothes and six loaded pistols, along with the $60,000 he picked up at the bank and an additional $50,000 which El Paso beer dealer George Baroody had given him some time before "for safekeeping." He took also two boxes of bank records which he did not dare to leave. In a car which he owned but which his father-in-law had been driving, he hit the road.

Where he went is still something of a mystery. He must have considered crossing into Mexico but fear of detection held him back. For six days he drove back and forth through Arizona and New Mexico, visiting Silver City and Tucson, where he had friends. Along the road near the latter place he cached the boxes of bank records behind some bushes. His mental condition deteriorated steadily.

Meanwhile the bank officers were backtracking him. A telephone call revealed that President McDonald of the Van Horn State Bank was not even in Texas on Tuesday, March 18. He and his wife were in New York.

It was at this point that Lockhart's resignation was announced. Southwestern law-enforcement agencies were alerted and the FBI was called in, but for four days there was no trace of the missing president.

The case ended in a Lordsburg motel on Monday, March 26. The final act was arranged with some care, the stage manager being R. R. Davis of Silver City, a dealer in mining machinery who had been a patron of the bank for over forty years and a long-time friend of Lockhart's. He was apparently in touch with the fugitive and persuaded him to submit to arrest. About nine p.m. on Sunday, March 24, the two men drove up to the Bel Shore motel in a Thunderbird and rented a double room. Next morning Davis was gone but Lockhart was still there. In the afternoon FBI men from

El Paso and Police Chief Tommy Ryan of Silver City arrived and took charge of Lockhart, his firearms and his suitcase full of money. He made no resistance and seemed to be expecting the officers.

The wheels of legal machinery began to turn in familiar, leisurely rhythm. There was a hearing before U. S. Commissioner Irving Israel in Deming and conferences between John Otto of Alamogordo and John A. Langford of El Paso, Lockhart's attorneys. Lockhart himself was moved first to Las Cruces and then to Albuquerque. Dr. George F. Schlenker, an El Paso psychiatrist, visited him briefly in the Las Cruces jail on Tuesday evening, March 27.

That same day the National Surety Company, the bonding firm, was awarded a writ of garnishment giving the officials first claim on the money in the suitcase. On that same day also the directors of The State National Bank met and elected George Matkin president in place of Robert A. Lockhart, resigned. Matkin kept his chairmanship of the board. The announcement contained this comment:

> Mr. Matkin served as president of the bank for eighteen years. Under his guidance the bank achieved outstanding growth while contributing significant leadership and direction to the progress of our city. We are gratified that Mr. Matkin has consented to resume the presidency.
>
> This is the time to look forward to the challenge of the future. Some exciting days are ahead. . . . We expect to make other major announcements in the next few months reflecting the tremendous dynamic growth of the bank. We are on the move.

On Wednesday there was a hearing before United States Commissioner Robert McCoy of Albuquerque in the course of which Dr. George Schlenker's tentative conclusions were reported by Attorney Otto: Lockhart, Schlenker said, was incompetent "to cooperate with his counsel, or to understand the nature of proceedings against him, or even to consent to removal" to El Paso.

McCoy halted the hearing at once and set the following Monday as the date for a competency hearing. Lockhart was taken to a cell in the Bernalillo County jail.

The hearing established the fact that he was a very sick man. Dr. Schlenker, supported by Dr. John McCarthy of Albuquerque, testified that Robert Lockhart was mentally unfit to stand trial.

McCarthy called him "a manic depressive type with possible neurological damage, extremely nervous and highly excitable. His entire pattern is psychotic."

Schlenker voiced the sadness that all felt for this wreck of a man "of exceptional substance."

Judge H. Vearle Payne concluded the hearing by committing Lockhart to the custody of the Attorney General for transfer to the Federal Medical Center at Springfield, Missouri, there to undergo treatment until "mentally competent to stand trial or charges against him are disposed of according to law."

Meanwhile back at the bank a thorough audit was under way to determine how much double dealing had actually gone on over the preceding five years. It was a time of great embarrassment to all concerned, but the officers and directors felt that no concealment could be tolerated. The public was naturally interested, but all employees behaved with great discretion. They realized that any revelations would have to come from Mr. Matkin and that it would be necessary for everybody else to go about his business cheerfully, calmly – and silently. It was obvious to them, and to everybody who knew anything at all about the bank, that it would take more than the failure of one man, even a president, to shake the State National.

There was more embarrassment to come. The investigators turned up evidence that Lockhart was not the only one who had abused his trust. On April 18, less than a month after Lockhart's flight, Hal B. Stewart, a State National assistant vice-president, was discharged from his employment. In a matter of hours, it was known all over town that he too was short in his accounts. The facts came out when a federal grand jury indicted him on July 2 for embezzlement of the bank's funds. The following day he turned himself in to Deputy U. S. Marshal James Johnson and appeared before U. S. Commissioner Fred Morton, who released him on a $5,000 surety bond.

Stewart was another of the bank's bright young men who had apparently begun a promising career. He had been promoted from assistant cashier to assistant vice-president in 1962, and at the time of his downfall he was head of the Loan and Discount Department.

In this position his opportunities to go astray were unusual, and his temptations were correspondingly strong. He had misappropriated over $70,000 between 1962 and 1969 – all spent on living beyond his means. There was no connection between his peculations and Lockhart's.

Through the summer and fall of 1969 the final acts in this drama of sin and retribution were played in El Paso courtrooms. Lockhart was returned from Missouri by way of Albuquerque on July 10. Ninety days in the federal hospital had restored him to something like a normal condition. On July 30 he was declared mentally competent to stand trial and pleaded innocent to the three indictments in his case. On the same day Stewart declared himself innocent of the nineteen charges returned against him by the grand jury. Judge D. W. Suttle set September 8 as the date of trial for both men.

On September 4, however, new charges were introduced against Lockhart – eight of them, detailing his embezzlement of $23,000 of bank funds in addition to the sums in his possession when he fled. Judge Suttle postponed the trial to September 20.

On that date Lockhart pleaded guilty to three of the eight counts in the second set of charges and on October 2 was sentenced to fifteen years in prison with no recommendation for an early parole. Stewart likewise pleaded guilty to three counts out of those lodged against him and in his turn was sentenced to ten years with possibility of early release.

And there the matter rested, and still rests.

Not since Mr. Morehead "retired" in 1921 have the officers, directors and friends of the bank endured so much embarrassment and grief. No money, of course, was lost, but the revelation of human weakness in the bank's citadel was a severe shock. There was, however, one ray of light: no appreciable change occurred in the volume of business – proof that the people of El Paso had not withdrawn their trust.

NEW BLOOD

• THE LOCKHART CASE was an ill wind that blew some good into The State National Bank. Actually it started a revolution.

After the blow fell, a complete review of the bank's records was necessary, and the firm of Peat, Marwick and Mitchell was engaged to undertake this monumental task. A flying corps of accountants moved in, displacing a good many officers who cheerfully followed their desks into odd corners and passageways. As the investigation went forward, the search for a new president got under way simultaneously. It seemed obvious to Matkin and to the officers and directors that the traditional policy of promotion from within the ranks would have to be abandoned – that the new chief executive would have to come from outside the bank.

Many good men were nominated and considered for the post, but the name which finally emerged at the head of the list was that of B. Glen Jordan, an internationally known management specialist with headquarters in New York City.

It made a difference that Jordan was a native of West Texas living in exile in the asphalt jungle. His BBA was from the University of Houston and he had joined the staff of the Bank of the Southwest in that city in 1946, rising to the rank of vice-president and assuming the responsibilities of general auditor and head of Accounting and Systems Planning. From Houston he went to St. Louis and a position with the important firm of Peat, Marwick and Mitchell. In 1969 he was in charge of their bank-management program with offices in New York. Just before coming to El Paso, he was working with management problems in Mexico, Peru, Brazil and Puerto Rico, as well as in the United States.

A man of so much capacity and such wide experience needed some convincing before he was willing to narrow his horizon to a bank in a medium-sized city on the Mexican border. Tad Smith, attorney for the bank, is given credit for persuading him that the State National was a challenge and an opportunity – a "sleeping giant" which a man of his capabilities could awaken. He had had nearly enough of the peripatetic life of a consultant, however, and was ready to stay in one place for a while. Besides, Texas was home. He was promised a free rein and the solid backing of the senior officers, and after a period of soul searching, he accepted the challenge. In January, 1970, he became the new president of El Paso's oldest bank.

The staff and the community recognized at once that he was a man superlatively well qualified for the job – tops in his field, a convincing speaker, an effective writer, an expert teacher, analyst, and organizer. His persuasiveness was soon a legend in the bank. "Glen is such a super-salesman," said Lynwood Boyer, a new executive, in an interview, "that he talked me into joining the bank after I had been here three months."[1]

Changes began at once, but they were not violent changes. Jordan has remarked to his friends that his most valuable contributions in other banks sometimes involved persuading the president to take a year or two for necessary reforms instead of ordering them into operation the following Monday. He knew the value of a loyal and dedicated staff and had no intention of undermining the *esprit de corps* of his new associates.

One of his first major decisions was to bring in an expert in organization to survey the bank's internal workings and make suggestions for improvement. The man he chose for this important job was Lynwood J. Boyer of Houston, who came to the bank on a three-months assignment in March of 1970.

Boyer was a Texan by adoption. He graduated from Penn State University as a chemical engineer and spent some time at Lackland and Ellington Air Force Bases as an aviation cadet in pilot training. Houston looked good to him and he returned there, to the Bank of the Southwest, when he got out of the Service. As a banker, he felt that he needed more education and took a degree in Economics and Finance at the University of Houston. During his ten years at the Bank of the Southwest, he came to know Glen Jordan. They were congenial and much alike in their views and methods, and it was natural that after Glen had left to join a consulting firm, he should wish to work with his old associate. In 1965 Boyer left Houston to become a traveling consultant specializing in banking problems and traveled from job to job in the Midwest and the East. Two years of living in motels and hotels was enough, however, and he returned to Houston, where he combined consulting (in Panama and Puerto Rico) with the presidency of a computer-leasing company. In due course his ties in Houston loosened, and about the same time, Glen Jordan decided to come to El Paso. Boyer joined him soon after – in March of 1970. In June he accepted a position in the bank as Vice-president and Manager of the Administration Division.

"Feeling about Glen the way I do," he told an interviewer, "and his capabilities and what he can do in a given situation if given the right tools and the right environment, I felt that it looked like a real opportunity and an interesting sort of situation."

Boyer thought of himself as primarily a specialist in people and human relations, but his experience had included special training in handling organizational problems. One of his jobs in the bank was to examine carefully its internal workings and set up a time table for constructive changes. His first assignment was to look for obvious and easily repaired loopholes in the bank's organization – for instance, whether there were too many tellers on the payroll – and he went on to more complicated problems. By August of 1970 he was completing a study of data processing and its possible uses in the bank. First he applied computer techniques to the internal workings of the organization and then surveyed their usefulness in marketing. It seemed to him that new industries might be attracted to this area if the bank would set up a "well operated computer center." Intelligent long-range planning was his goal.[2] The bank and its operations were to be under frequent scrutiny; efforts to improve procedures were to be constant.

The Administrative Division was one of five which replaced the old departments. The others were Trust, Marketing, Loan, Planning and Control. The idea was to streamline the organization, clarify the chain of command, free executive officers from responsibilities which ought to belong to somebody else and allow them to concentrate on the responsibilities that were rightfully theirs.

George G. Matkin
Chairman of the Board

B. Glen Jordan
President

Harrison M. Daugherty, Sr.
Advisory Director of the Board

E. Guyler Magruder
Vice President

Walter W. Scott
Vice President and Trust Officer

Chris P. Fox
Vice President
Director of Public Relations

Vice Presidents and Managers of the Bank's Five Departments

From the left: Martin Kern, *Trust;* Lynwood J. Boyer, *Administrative;* Tom Foster, *Loan;* William M. Updike, *Marketing;* J. Gordon Johnson, *Planning & Control.*

The new Trust Officer, Vice President Martin Kern, was particularly concerned about wasted time and energy. "One of the sources of duplication of effort and of general inefficiency," he remarked on assuming his new position, "is that everybody has been involved in Operations. Everything apart from the decision-making process in a sense becomes Operations – day-to-day activities. So we are going to break this out and have an Operations Department with somebody in charge. Ideally, when this is functioning, our Trust administrators will have time enough to administrate. It takes our investment people out of the functional operational part so they can devote their time entirely to making decisions about investments. When they make a decision and a broker has been called and a stock has been bought, they don't have to worry about the clearance and getting it paid for and getting it transferred."[3]

Kern was one of the comparatively young men with good potential who were moved up in the course of the reorganization. A man of multiple talents – writer, musician, financial specialist – he graduated from Ohio State University with a major in English literature. During World War II he was a member of an Air Force heavy bomber group. His best friend in the Service was Granville Mott, well known in El Paso as a public-relations and advertising man until his untimely death in 1969. Kern and Mott wrote a play involving their war experiences in the Air Force. After the Armistice was signed Mott returned to El Paso; Kern got a job in New York writing for a business magazine and spent his spare time trying to market the play. He never quite succeeded, but he came close, and he picked up some valuable experience. In 1947 he came to El Paso to visit Granville and never got around to leaving.

He made all or part of his living for a while as a professional pianist, but after he accumulated a family, neither his piano nor his free-lance work for local advertising agencies seemed enough like a steady job, so he went to work for Sarah Freese and stayed with her stock-brokerage firm for thirteen years. By that time he "needed a little more information" and spent a year and a half at the University of California, coming out with a Master of Business Administration. George Matkin had encouraged him to apply at the bank when he finished, and in August of 1965 he signed on as a securities analyst.

One of his first steps after taking charge of the Trust Division was to free the trust officers, as much as possible, from any service as public financial consultants. This required some effort and much diplomacy, for many customers who trusted the bank above all other earthly agencies had long made a practice of dropping in for free advice about investments. "You cannot really serve the dual function," Martin once remarked in this connection. "Our primary responsibility is to the trust accounts and we are not staffed adequately to serve in other ways. Moreover, it's very expensive to provide this service. There will be a Customers' Service Department in the new bank with a big block of space for investment services. It will be a multiple-purpose thing, but it will go out of Trust entirely."

Early in his involvement with the Trust Department, Martin came to realize that "there is a great potential market that hasn't been touched. Sometimes people need a service and don't know they need it." Once the Trust Division is able to concentrate on Trust business, in his view, it can do a better job of building the right image in places where it counts and finding ways to let potential customers know how the Trust officers can serve them.

Another division, with William M. Updike in charge, was set up to handle marketing. Several special activities and about five departments were brought together under this divisional umbrella: Public Relations, National Accounts and Correspondent Banks, Business Development, the Officer Call Program, Bank Americard activities, Industrial Development, and the International Department. The word *marketing* in this context involves promoting—selling—the services of the bank. Most agencies which help in any way to spread the gospel of the SNB are in the Marketing Division.

At the time of his appointment Bill Updike, in comparison with his fellow division heads, was an old El Paso hand, though he had been with the bank only a year when his job was created. He came to town shortly after World War II as an employee of General Electric, bringing a degree from Carleton College, Northfield, Minnesota. His first involvement with the banking business was a job at the El Paso National Bank, where he served for thirteen years. He was "primarily loan oriented," but he had learned about all the other bank services by the time those thirteen years were up. "We have great hopes for our International Department," he said in the summer of 1970. "Banking relations with Mexico, especially, offer many opportunities. The Industrial Development service is another with great possibilities. There is a tremendous amount of interest in El Paso. Many people are looking at the area. The 'Twin Plant' concept is a prime mover to get people to come down here. Interest has been great during the last couple of years. Whether or not our visitors go in for the Twin Plant concept, if we can get them to El Paso, we can sell them on the town. The Hallicrafters Company came in six months ago, and their growth has been fantastic. These people are doing in El Paso now what I saw in plants in New Jersey and New York fifteen or eighteen years ago. I remember saying to myself, 'That's what they ought to be doing down here on account of our labor supply and so on.' "[4]

An important part of Updike's division is the Industrial Development service, headed by Bob Chaplin, young and energetic, who came to El Paso with an appointment as Assistant Professor of Economics at UTEP. Both Bob and his wife are bilingual, their Spanish being good enough to take them through a two-year appointment at the University of Guadalajara. Bob's job as Bank Economist is to watch what goes on in business on both sides of the border and help the bank to adjust its policies to new developments.

The Loan Division became the responsibility of Thomas R. Foster, an employee of the bank since 1946. Tom was born at Denison, Texas, went through the public schools, and served during the Second World War in the Naval Submarine Service. He began his banking career as a bookkeeper in the old, traditional way, but he made every effort to add to his skills and information, earning the Advanced Certificate of the American Institute of Banking in 1959 and graduating from the Southwest School of Banking at Southern Methodist University in 1965. As Vice-president and Manager of the Loan Division, his real function is to oversee the work of ten vice-presidents, four assistant vice-presidents, and three assistant cashiers. His experience and firmness of character, combined with his natural courtesy and diplomacy entitle him to the top job in his division.

The Planning and Control Division, last to be organized, was placed in charge of J. Gordon Johnson in December, 1970. An El

Paso boy with an M.A. in Accounting from U. T. Austin, Johnson has "stature, ability and experience," according to President Jordan.[5]

A new vice-president who came into the bank with a strong personal interest was Hal Daugherty, Jr., son of the vice-chairman of the board. A grandson of C. N. Bassett, he determined on a banking career early in life and after graduating from the Taft School in Connecticut, he went on to the Wharton School of Finance to prepare himself for his future occupation. The next stop was the First National Bank of Dallas, where he finished the officer-training program and went to work first as a credit analyst and then as a loan officer. After six and a half years in Dallas, he was called home to help with the housecleaning and rebuilding which followed the Lockhart tragedy.

Like the other officers, he feels that the bank is on the verge of a great new day. "We were lucky to get Glen Jordan," he says. "He has brought a new fresh outlook to the bank. The knowledge and expertise he has brought to us makes the Lockhart affair almost a blessing in disguise."[6]

"Glen is a remarkable man," Bill Updike adds. "I think if we had a choice of anyone in the country to come out here and head up the bank, it would be Glen Jordan."

The revolution, as all the officers know, is serious business. There has never been the least doubt what it involves. Jordan tells his lieutenants what he expects of them, and they know that they will have to deliver or be replaced. At the same time, they know that along with the responsibility, they have all the authority they need to get the job done.[7] A good man never asks for more.

"For me personally." Martin Kern declares, "this is a very exciting time. I get my pants on in the morning and I can't wait to get down here. And that's pretty good, you know. I feel very confident about the future of the Trust Division and of the bank. I think five years from now, it's going to be a model bank. I mean a *model* bank!"

In 1971 the future of the State National looks bright. George Matkin's colleagues give him full credit for the surge forward. It was his wisdom and adaptability which turned the tide and brought potential victory out of seeming defeat.

CHAPTER XV

TALLEST BANK IN TOWN

• IF 1970 WAS THE YEAR OF REVOLUTION, 1971 will be remembered as the year of realization – the year of the move to the State National's fine new home, its fifth, counting temporary quarter in 1921-22. When Mr. Morehead and Mr. Austin opened for business in Major Fewel's new brick building in 1881, they could not have dreamed that ninety years later the bank's physical plant would occupy the better part of a downtown block and would include an office tower rising 286 feet and twenty-two stories above the pavement.

A project as big as this one, probably good for another century, could not be put together in a hurry. The dream of many years finally reached the planning stage, and the preliminary studies were not rushed. For almost two years after a firm decision was made, nobody in the bank could or would say much about what developments were taking place. The officers felt that it would be useless to make announcements until there was something positive to announce.

One thing they would admit: the move to new quarters would be, in a way, a homecoming. The site selected was the block bounded by Stanton, Mills and Kansas Streets where O. T. Bassett had established his lumber business in 1881 and commenced building El Paso. The entire block has belonged to the Bassett family ever since and is the one right place for the State National's new headquarters.

Considerable downtown history has unfolded at or near the corner of Mills and Stanton. When the lumber yard was moved, a business block took its place. There were stores and shops below and lodgings above – first the Bassett Flats and the Lake House; then the Lockie Hotel. In 1951 the building was completely remodeled and renamed the 1881 Building, commemorating the far-reaching changes that began in that year.

The northeast corner of the block, at Mills and Kansas Streets, was the site of one of El Paso's first skating rinks and later of the old Auditorium Garage. It was a parking lot in 1969.

The management made sure that the best talent in the United States was called in to assist in the planning and building. The Ogden Development Corporation of Los Angeles signed on as joint owner of the office tower. Ogden specializes in all phases of its business — site acquisition, economic and social research as a basis for planning, architecture, engineering, financing, supervision of construction, leasing and management. The phrase used by the company to describe its multiple approach is "total competency."

The architects who planned the complex are also nationally and internationally known: Charles Luckman Associates of Los Angeles, New York, Boston and Phoenix. Luckman did the planning for the new Madison Square Garden in New York, the Los Angeles Forum, the Manned Spacecraft Center in Houston, the Prudential Center in Boston, the Stanford Linear Accelerator Center. The firm has designed convention centers, stadiums and office buildings in Los Angeles, Honolulu, Cleveland, Pittsburgh, Phoenix and Palm Springs.

The firm of Kuykendall, McCombs, Middleton and Staten were the local architects on the job.

By May, 23, 1969, so much progress had been made that the bank officials felt the time had arrived for a public announcement, and they called in representatives of local news media for a press conference. Members of the Board of Directors, officers of the bank, and a few friends gathered in the Director's Room to hear the good news. A large colored picture of the new bank and office tower was displayed on an easel. George Matkin, President and Chairman of the Board, opened the session, concluding his remarks as follows:

> I hope you will concur with us, as you see the architect's rendering of our new building, that it will be a really great asset both architecturally and from a utility standpoint to downtown El Paso, and a decided addition to the El Paso skyline. We are very excited about it, and we look forward to its completion and many wonderful years of living in it. We are going into this project with the thought that El Paso will continue to grow and prosper, and The State National Bank will do likewise.

Through the months that followed, preparations for the new structures went forward step by step. First the 1881 Building came down, leaving a vacancy in the center of town which affected the citizens like a missing tooth. Passersby often stopped to gaze at the wreckage as if they could not quite believe their eyes.

By the end of December, 1969, the contract for construction was ready to be signed. Two nationally-known building firms with headquarters in El Paso – C. H. Leavell and Company and Robert E. McKee, General Contractor, Inc. – agreed to make the contract a joint venture.

This was a real surprise. The two companies had long been rivals. They were both good customers of the bank, however, and their bids were so close that President Matkin called them in and proposed a joint effort. They agreed; and Matkin was heard to say that the biggest break-through in setting up plans was getting Leavell and McKee together. The contract was signed before photographers in the State National's Board Room on December 23, 1969.

Construction began as soon as the clearing of the site was finished early in 1970. Completion was scheduled for the fall of 1971. Sidewalk superintendents watched as giant augers bored holes for the steel caissons and eight-foot-long anchor bolts which would tie the office tower to the earth. There was so much interest that Chris Fox, in charge of public relations, issued a humorously worded Sidewalk Superintendent Permit entitling the bearer to watch all he wanted to.

Dedication ceremonies were held on January 30, 1970, with the Bassett family and the officers of the bank in attendance, and before long steel began to emerge from the excavation. Plans included a Motorbank which was to rise on the block east of the main structure. When work began on the tunnel which was to connect the two buildings, traffic on Kansas Street had to be rerouted, but nobody complained. Watching the bank grow was watching El Paso grow.

In full-page newspaper advertisements the SNB let every El Pasoan know the vital statistics of the new plant. Compared with any of the banks in Mr. Morehead's time, the scale is enormous. The one-story lobby measures 105x150 feet. No columns support the twenty-four-foot ceiling. A clear-span lobby of this size is almost unique in the Southwest.

The plans locate the office tower in the eastern half of the block with plenty of clear space around it on all four sides. "It opens up the heart of the business district," according to the architect's description, "to air and light and planted beauty." Bronze window walls break the great expanses of metallic sheathing. The windows themselves are of bronze-tinted glass. A glass-enclosed passageway connects the tower with the bank lobby and the Kansas Street tunnel conducts clients from the 600-car parking garage above the Motorbank to the business area. The State National intends to be the most progressive bank in town. Its home, for a good many years to come, will be the tallest building.

While the contractors were excavating and pouring and welding the new building together, the officers had to make some far-reaching decisions. They had to make up their minds whether they wanted to stay at normal speed or shift into overdrive. The old bank was already bursting at its bronze-and-marble seams. Should the revolution and reorganization be completed when new quarters provided the needed room, or should everything be shaped up and ready when it was time to make the move? The management decided that it was best to be organized and ready.

"We don't want to wait till the new bank is built," Lynwood Boyer summarized after construction had started. "We don't want to play musical chairs on the weekend that we move. We are going to get this big, squeaky wheel moving. We are going to make the changes now, even though we are physically cramped, and will start operating as we will be operating in the new building. Hopefully, as a result of this, we will cut maybe two years off any schedule that might have been in existence before. So far as growth is concerned, we are going to hit the new building running and use it as a springboard into our future development."

That is a good sample of the spirit of the State National in 1971.

If the pace can be maintained, what will the situation be in 1981, the centennial year?

Hopefully, when a newcomer asks in that year, "Which is the model bank of the Southwest?" the right answer will be the words of the SNB's old familiar slogan, in use since 1952:

THE STATE NATIONAL, OF COURSE!

The New Building at the time of the publication of this book.

[The tower rises 22 stories above the site of the old Bassett Lumber Company. The large crane at left center is working on the SNB Motor Bank and Parking Garage.]

[TED COLLINS]

SOURCES

BOOKS AND ARTICLES

John Vinson Barton, *El Paso in 1890*. M. A. Thesis, Texas Western College, 1963.

W.W. Bridgers, *Just Chatting* (Typescript). 4 vols. El Paso Public Library.

Richard H. Burges Collection (Scrapbooks). Mrs. Jane B. Perrenot.

Robert N. Burns, "The Newman Brothers: Forgotten Cattle Kings of the Northern Plains." *Montana* XI (October, 1961), 28-36.

Avery Luvere Carlson, *A Monetary and Banking History of Texas . . . 1821-1929*. Fort Worth: Fort Worth National Bank, 1930.

Sanford Cox, *The State National Bank*. History Seminar Paper, Texas Western College, 1952.

William Elsey Connelley, *Doniphan's Expedition and the Conquest of New Mexico and California*. Kansas City, Mo.: Bryant Book and Stationery Company, 1907 (Biographical material on C. R. Morehead).

Frank V. Dearing, ed., *The Best Novels and Stories of Eugene Manlove Rhodes*. Boston: Houghton, Mifflin, 1949.

El Paso Chamber of Commerce, Report for 1911.

El Paso City Council Minutes, Book B (1880).

El Paso County Board of Development, *The Changing Face of El Paso*. El Paso, 1966.

Pioneer Association of El Paso, *Sketchbook*, MS. The University of Texas at El Paso Library.

El Paso Industrial Development Corporation, *This Is El Paso*. El Paso, 1967.

El Paso Industrial Development Corporation, *El Paso Area Fact Book*. El Paso, 1968.

El Paso Weather Bureau, Records, 1880-90.

J. Evetts Haley, *Jeff Milton, a Good Man with a Gun*. Norman: University of Oklahoma Press, 1948.

Asbury Harpending, *The Great Diamond Hoax*. Norman: University of Oklahoma Press, 1957.

Mildred L. Jordan, *Railroads in the El Paso Area*. M. A. Thesis, Texas Western College, 1957.

Walter Kohlberg, *A Translation of the Letters Written by Ernest Kohlberg, 1875, 1876, 1877* (MS, copy in possession of Mrs. Leonard Goodman).

Lydia Spencer Lane, *I Married a Soldier*. Albuquerque: Horn and Wallace, 1964 (original publication, 1893).

William E. Leuchtenburg, *Franklin D. Roosevelt and the New Deal 1932-1940*. New York: Harper and Row, 1963.

Bill McGaw, "El Paso National Bank Founder . . . Goes Mad when Bank Fails." *The Southwesterner* VI (May, 1967), 1, 10, 12-13.

Richard K. McMaster, *Musket, Saber and Missile: A History of Fort Bliss*. El Paso: Complete Printing and Letter Service, 1962.

James Graham McNary, *This Is My Life*. Albuquerque: University of New Mexico Press, 1956.

James Marshall, *Elbridge A. Stuart: Founder of Carnation Company*. Los Angeles: Western Printing and Lithographing Company, 1949.

Mary Jean Martin, *C. E. Kelly: Mayor of El Paso 1910-1915*. History Seminar paper, Texas Western College, 1956.

Leon C. Metz, *Dallas Stoudenmire*. Austin: Pemberton Press, 1969.

John Middagh, *Frontier Newspaper: The El Paso Times*. El Paso: Texas Western Press, 1958.

Anson Mills, *My Story*. Washington: Byron S. Adams, 1921 (second edition).

W. W. Mills, *Forty Years at El Paso 1858-1898* (ed. Rex W. Strickland). El Paso: Carl Hertzog, 1962 (original copyright, 1901).

C. R. Morehead, *Diary*. Original in possession of Mrs. Dexter Mapel; copy in El Paso Public Library.

C. R. Morehead, *Early Days on the Far Western Plains*. El Paso Pioneer Tells of His Experiences (typescript, El Paso Public Library).

Leonora Mosier, *History of the El Paso Fire Department 1882-1910*. History Seminar Paper, Texas Western College, 1956.

S. H. Newman, *Reminiscenses* (MS). Copy in possession of S. H. Newman III.

Tom B. Newman, *History of the Newman Family up to 1961* (MS). Copy in possession of S. H. Newman III.

Joe Parrish, "Hanged by the Neck." *Password* III (April, 1958), 72, 75.

Robert T. Patterson, *The Great Boom and Panic 1921-1929*. Chicago: Henry Regnery, 1965.

J. D. Ponder, "Charles R. Morehead Was Leader of Men, Says J. D. Ponder." El Paso *Times*, December 18, 1921.

Patricia Reschenthaler, *Postwar Growth in El Paso 1945-1950*. El Paso: Texas Western Press, 1968.

John M. Richards, *Economic Growth in El Paso 1950-1962*. El Paso Bureau of Business and Economic Research, Texas Western College, 1964.

Donald B. Sanger, *The Story of Old Fort Bliss*. El Paso: Privately Printed, 1933.

Arthur M. Schlesinger, Jr., *The Coming of the New Deal (The Age of Roosevelt, II)*. Boston: Houghton, Mifflin, 1959.

John Selman, Jr., *John Selman of El Paso* (MS). Copy in possession of Leon C. Metz.

Edward C. Sherman, *The Ku Klux Klan and El Paso Politics following World War I*. History Seminar Paper, Texas Western College, August, 1958.

Kimball C. Smith, *History of Banking in El Paso* (MS).

C. L. Sonnichsen, *The El Paso Salt War*. El Paso: Carl Hertzog and Texas Western Press, 1961.

The State National Bank of El Paso, Articles of Association (Record Books, A).

The State National Bank of El Paso, Minutes of the Board of Directors.

The State National Bank of El Paso, Scrapbooks.

M. H. Thomlinson, *The Garrison of Fort Bliss*. El Paso: Hertzog and Resler, 1945.

Dr. Howard Thompson, *Builders of El Paso* (typescript), 1945.

Jack Vowell, *Politics in El Paso 1850-1920*. M. A. Thesis, Texas Western College, 1950.

John L. Waller, "Colonel George Wythe Baylor." *Southwestern Social Science Quarterly* XXIV (June, 1943), 23-35.

Walter Prescott Webb, *The Texas Rangers*. Boston: Houghton, Mifflin, 1935.

Dixon Wecter, *The Age of the Great Depression 1929-1941*. New York: Macmillan, 1948.

Paul I. Wellman, *The Indian Wars of the West*. Garden City: Doubleday, 1954.

Alice M. White, *History of the Development of Irrigation in the El Paso Valley*. M. A. Thesis, Texas Western College, 1950.

Owen White, *The Autobiography of a Durable Sinner*. New York: Putnam, 1942.

Owen White, *Out of the Desert: the Historical Romance of El Paso*. El Paso: The McMath Company, 1924.

Gladys Williams, *Orchestras and Bands: El Paso Music 1880-1960*. M. A. Thesis, Texas Western College, 1960.

Neill C. Wilson and Frank J. Taylor, *Southern Pacific*. New York: McGraw-Hill, 1952.

NEWSPAPERS

El Paso *Herald* and *Herald-Post*.

El Paso *Lone Star*.

El Paso *Times*.

El Paso *Evening Tribune*.

Home Town News (Mimeographed newssheet issued weekly by The State National Bank and sent to servicemen from El Paso).

INTERVIEWS

Raymond Adams, June 25, 1968.
James Alcorn, September 8, 1968.
Frances Arledge, January 10, 1969.
R. E. Austin, June 12, 1969.
Mrs. C. N. Bassett, July 30, 1968.
Lynwood Boyer, July 30, 1970.
Tom Brennan, July 19, 1968.
Riley Brown, June 13, 1968.
Jack Clark, July 30, 1968.
Myra Bassett Daugherty, August 28, 1968.
H. M. Daugherty, July 19, 23, August 28, 1968; August 17, 1970.
H. M. Daugherty, Jr., July 24, 1970.
Thomas R. Foster, January 15, 1969.
Kenneth Gifford, August 28, 1968.
William Hanley, July 26, 1968.
Thornton Hardie, January 22, 1961.
Freeman Harris, June 13, 1968.
Joe Herrera, July 8, 1968; July 24, 1970.
Carl Hertzog, January 21, 1970.
Sidney Howard, August 26, 1968.
B. Glen Jordan, July 14, 1970.
Martin Kern, July 30, 1970.
Robert Lockhart, July 8, 1968.
E. Guyler Magruder, July 5, 9, September 27, 1968.
Charles McKay, July 16, 1968.
Mrs. Dexter Mapel, September 20, 1968.
George Matkin, June 28, July 9, September 27, 1968; August 18, 1970.
Jack Moore, January 10, 1969.
E. Bert Neugebauer, July 16, 1968.
Charles O'Hara, January 22, 1961.
Constance Pateman, January 27, 1970.
Pearl Ponsford, January 24, 1961.
William Purse, July 8, 1968.
Mrs. Addie Ross, June 4, 1968.
Doris Ryan, July 23, 1968.
Walter W. Scott, June 1, 15, 1969; August 6, 1970.
Lawrence R. Shea, August 6, 1970.
Kimball C. Smith, June 26, 1968.
Laurence Stevens, April 2, 1965.
William M. Updike, July 24, 1970.
Mrs. W. W. Wimberly, June 10, 1968.

REFERENCES

CHAPTER I

The Birth of a Bank

1 Weather Bureau records, El Paso, Texas.

2 The *Diary of C. R. Morehead,* MS. Morehead's private record for this period, now in possession of Mrs. Dexter Mapel, his granddaughter, has been transcribed and placed in the El Paso Public Library. It is used by courtesy of Mrs. Mapel and Librarian John Wayne Smith. Mr. Morehead's life story was included in the *National Cyclopedia of American Biography* and reproduced in William Elsey Connelley's *Doniphan's Expedition.* Additional details come from the El Paso *Herald-Post,* April 28, 1956 ("Men of Vision Founded City's Oldest Bank") and the El Paso *Times* for December 16, 1921 (obituary notice). J. D. Ponder added information in the El Paso *Times* for December 18, 1921.

3 Webb, *The Texas Rangers,* 398-399.

4 Mrs. Dexter Mapel, El Paso, September 20, 1968.

5 Connelley, *Doniphan's Expedition,* quoting *National Cyclopedia of American Biography.*

6 J. D. Ponder, "Charles R. Morehead Was Leader of Men," El Paso *Times,* December 18, 1921.

7 Dr. Howard Thompson, *Builders of El Paso,* MS.

8 Mrs. Dexter Mapel; C. R. Morehead, *Early Days on the Far Western Plains* (typescript).

9 Simeon H. Newman III of El Paso (grandson of Editor S. H. Newman of the El Paso *Lone Star*) has gathered much material on the Newman family and made it available to CLS and MGM: Robert H. Burns, "The Newman Brothers: Forgotten Cattle Kings of the Northern Plains," *Montana* XI (Autumn, 1961), 28-36; letter from Mrs. Edith Newman Reynolds, *Ibid.,* 32; El Paso *Times,* Nov-

ember 2, 1941 (obituary notice of C. M. Newman); *Ibid.*, February 23, 1911 (obituary notice of H. L. Newman); Tom B. Newman, *History of the Newman Family up to1961*, MS.

10 Mrs. Dexter Mapel; Myra Bassett Daugherty, August 28, 1968.

11 Morehead, *Diary*.

12 H. L. Newman to Comptroller of the Currency, January 29, 1880, copy in possession of K. C. Smith, El Paso.

13 *Ibid.*

14 Morehead, *Diary*.

15 White, *Out of the Desert*, 165.

16 Morehead, *Diary*.

17 El Paso *Times*, June 5, 1890.

18 George Matkin, July 9, 1968.

19 SNB Directors' Minutes, Book A.

20 *Times*, October 11, 1919.

21 The State National Bank Scrapbook.

CHAPTER II

Border Town

1 Mills, *Forty Years*, 18.

2 Kohlberg, *A Translation of the Letters Written By Ernest Kohlberg*, MS, describes one of these parties.

3 S. H. Newman, *Reminiscences*, MS.

4 Wilson and Taylor, *Southern Pacific*, 73-77.

5 Sonnichsen, *The Salt War*, tells the story.

6 Webb, *The Texas Rangers*, 403-406; Wellman, *The Indian Wars of the West*, 388-391.

7 Webb, *The Texas Rangers*, 403-406; Waller, "Colonel George Wythe Baylor," 32.

8 Mills, *Forty Years*, 5.

9 *Ibid.*, 69-70.

10 White, *Out of the Desert*, 108.

11 Jordan, *Railroads in the El Paso Area*, 149-151.

12 Marshall, *Elbridge A. Stewart*, 38-42.

13 Bridgers, *Just Chatting*, I, 202, 203.

14 John Selman, Jr., *John Selman of El Paso*, MS.

15 Gillett, *Six Years with the Texas Rangers*, 323.

16 El Paso City Council Minutes, Book B, July 31, 1880.

17 Metz, *Dallas Stoudenmire*, 34-44.

18 Middagh, *Frontier Newspaper*, 3.

CHAPTER III

The First Years

1 Carlson, *A Monetary and Banking History of Texas*, 7-10.

2 Smith, *History of Banking in El Paso*, MS.

3 Carlson, 21.

4 R. E. Stewart, Deputy Commissioner, Department of Banking, State of Texas, to M. G. McKinney, June 24, 1968.

5 Smith, *History of Banking*, MS.

6 At the close of business on December 31, 1881, The State National Bank listed resources of $229,550.57. The First National listed $248,627.59 (The State National Bank Scrapbook).

7 SNB Directors' Minutes, February 4, 1882.

8 *Ibid., January* 15, 1882; January 14, 1908.

9 W. W. Scott, June 4, 1968.

10 El Paso *Lone Star*, January 18, 1882.

11 *Ibid.*, September 4, 1882.

12 Records, El Paso Weather Bureau.

13 The State National Bank Scrapbook.

14 Mrs. Addie Ross, June 4, 1968.

15 The State National Bank Scrapbook.

16 George Matkin, July 9, 1968.

17 H. M. Daugherty, July 23, 1968.

18 *Lone Star*, September 5, 1883.

19 El Paso *Times*, May 16, 17, 1884.

20 *Ibid.*, May 18, 1884.

21 *Ibid.*, October 18, 1884.

22 *Ibid.*, April 14, 1885.

23 Owen White, *Autobiography*, 71, thinks the sinners did outnumber the good people and that "political control was in the hands of the vice element."

24 Tom B. Newman, *History of the Newman Family*, MS.

25 Copy in collection of K. C. Smith.

CHAPTER IV

Progress and Politics

1 Harpending, *The Great Diamond Hoax*, 171-178.

2 Bill McGaw, "El Paso National Bank Founder . . . Goes Mad. . . ." *The Southwesterner*, Vol. 6, May, 1967, 1, 10, 12-13.

3 El Paso *Times,* September 6, 1886.

4 W. H. Austin's application for charter, files of Comptroller of the Currency, copy in collection of K. C. Smith, El Paso.

5 El Paso *Lone Star,* April 11, May 19, August 1, 15, 1883; Vowell, *Politics in El Paso,* 84-86.

6 J. D. Ponder, "Charles R. Morehead Was Leader of Men. . . ." El Paso *Times,* December 18, 1921.

7 Lydia Spencer Lane, *I Married a Soldier,* 172.

8 City Council Minutes, Book B, July 31, 1880.

9 Mosier, *History of the El Paso Fire Department,* 5.

10 *Lone Star,* December 16, 1882.

11 *Ibid.*

12 *Times,* September 4, 6, 1886.

13 Vowell, *Politics in El Paso,* 86.

14 John Selman, Jr., *John Selman of El Paso,* MS.

15 *Lone Star,* August 11, 1883.

16 *Times,* November 11, 1888.

17 *Ibid.,* March 12,,1889.

18 *Ibid.,* March 17, 1889.

19 *Ibid.,* March 12, 1889.

20 *Ibid.,* March 19, 1889.

21 *Ibid.,* April 9, 1889.

22 *Ibid.,* March 20, 22, 1889.

23 *Ibid.,* April 10, 1889.

24 *Ibid.,* June 7, 1889.

25 *Ibid.,* April 18, 1889.

26 *Ibid.,* May 7, 8, 9, 1889.

27 *Ibid.,* March 14, 1889.

28 *Ibid.,* June 7, 1889.

Chapter V

The Second Decade

1 Statements of condition were published annually in the El Paso papers.

2 SNB Directors' Minutes, Book A.

3 W. W. Scott, August 9, 1968.

4 El Paso *Times,* April 20, 1898.

5 Williams, *Orchestras and Bands,* 4 ff.

6 For the McGinty Club see the El Paso *Herald,* July 17, 31, August 7, 14, 21, 28, September 4, 1909.

7 El Paso *Herald-Post,* July 29, 1947; *Times,* August 2, 1947.

8 *Autobiography of a Durable Sinner,* 71.

9 Webb, *The Texas Rangers,* 441-444.

10 Laurence Stevens, April 2, 1965.

11 *Herald,* April 18, 1890.

12 Parrish, "Hanged by the Neck," *Password* III (April, 1958), 72, 75.

13 Mills, *My Story,* 256-269; *Times,* January 2, 27, 1890; White, *History of Development of Irrigation,* 93-106.

14 Thomlinson, *The Garrison of Fort Bliss,* 29.

15 McMaster, *Musket, Saber and Missile,* 36; *Times,* July 24, 1890.

16 *Herald,* March 20, 1890.

17 *Times,* May 1, 1890.

18 *Ibid.,* June 4, 1890.

19 *Ibid.,* July 24, 1890.

20 Sanger, *The Story of Fort Bliss,* 17.

21 John Vinson Barton, *El Paso in 1890,* 45; *Times,* July 23, 1890.

22 *Times,* July 24, August 26, 1890.

23 *Ibid.,* August 26, 1890.

24 *Ibid.,* August 30, 1890.

25 Middagh, *Frontier Newspaper,* 119.

26 *Times,* June 11, 1890.

27 *Ibid.,* January 1, 1890.

28 *Ibid.*

29 *Times,* January 20, 1890.

30 *Ibid.,* February 24, 1890.

31 *Ibid.,* April 20, 1890.

32 *Ibid.,* November 15, 1892.

33 *Herald,* March 3, 1893.

34 The State National Bank Scrapbook, undated clipping.

35 *Times,* January 26, 1893.

36 *Ibid.,* January 14, 1890.

37 *Herald,* January 23, 25, 1893.

38 *Ibid.,* April 1, 1893.

39 *Times,* April 10, 1893.

40 *Ibid.,* February 21, 1893.

41 *Ibid.,* February 2, 1893.

42 *Herald,* April 12, 1893.

43 *Times,* August 3, 1893.

44 *Ibid.*

45 The State National Bank Scrapbook, undated clipping from the Albuquerque *Democrat.*

46 *Times,* October 13, 17, 1893.

47 El Paso *Tribune,* October 24, 1893.

48 The State National Bank Scrapbook, undated clipping.

49 Dr. Howard Thompson, *Builders of El Paso,* MS.

50 The State National Bank Scrapbook, undated clipping.

51 *Times,* May 16, 1909.
52 *Herald,* April 19, 1918.
53 Vowell, *Politics in El Paso,* tells the story.
54 Haley, *Jeff Milton,* 211-225.
55 *Herald,* April 10, 1895.
56 Vowell, *Politics,* 117.
57 *Herald,* April 5, 1899.
58 *Ibid.*
59 Myra Bassett Daugherty, August 28, 1968.
60 *Herald,* January 4, 1898.

CHAPTER VI

Under New Management

1 The material on Flory is pieced together from the recollections of George Matkin, H. M. Daugherty, Guyler Magruder, W. W. Scott, Myra Bassett Daugherty and others, and from newspaper accounts at the time of his death (El Paso *Herald-Post,* June 13, 14, 1932; El Paso *Times,* June 14, 1932).
2 Jack Moore, January 10, 1969.
3 H. M. Daugherty, July 19, 1968; George Matkin, June 28, 1968.
4 Mrs. C. N. Bassett, July 30, 1968; H. M. Daugherty.
5 Myra Bassett Daugherty, August 28, 1968.
6 *Ibid.*
7 *Ibid.*
8 George Matkin.
9 Flory's romantic involvements: Charles O'Hara and Thornton Hardie, January 22, 1961; Dr. Pearl Ponsford, January 24, 1961; Constance Pateman, January 27, 1970. Hertzog's saddle: Carl Hertzog, January 2, 1970.
10 Mrs. C. N. Bassett; *Times,* December 2, 1969.
11 W. W. Bridgers describes the rally: *Times,* May 12, 1946.
12 *Times,* September 1, 1904; *Herald,* July 9, March 19, 1904, May 12, 1906.
13 *Times,* September 17, 1904.
14 *Herald,* November 10, 11, 1904.
15 *Ibid.,* November 11, 1904.
16 *Ibid.,* November 11, 25, 1904.
17 *Times,* November 21, 1904.
18 *Ibid.,* November 26, 1904.
19 Martin, *C. E. Kelly,* tells the story.
20 Vowell, *Politics in El Paso,* 106.
21 *Herald,* November 9, 1905.
22 *Ibid.,* July 8, 1908.
23 El Paso *Times,* May 16, 1919; *Herald,* May 16, 1919; Guyler Magruder, September 27, 1968; George Matkin, September 28, 1968.
24 George Matkin, June 28, 1968.
25 Guyler Magruder, July 5, 1968.
26 Mrs. C. N. Bassett.
27 George Matkin, June 28, 1968.
28 J. D. Ponder, "Charles R. Morehead Was Leader of Men," *Times,* December 18, 1921.

CHAPTER VII

Crisis

1 SNB Directors' Minutes, October 1, 1920.
2 Jack Clark, July 30, 1968; Walter Scott, August 6, 1970.
3 W. W. Scott, June 12, 1968.
4 El Paso *Herald,* January 28, 29, 1922.
5 William Hanley, July 26, 1968.
6 *Herald,* January 28, 29, 1922.
7 SNB Board of Directors' Minutes. January 13, 1920; January 13, 1925.
8 For the Ku Klux Klan see John Middagh's *Frontier Newspaper,* Ch. XV, and Edward F. Sherman's *The Ku Klux Klan and El Paso Politics.*
9 George Matkin, Walter Scott and H. M. Daugherty, December 27, 1968.
10 Guyler Magruder, July 5, 1968.
11 George Matkin, July 9, 1968.
12 *Ibid.*
13 El Paso *Times,* September 4, 1931.
14 *Ibid.,* September 5, 1931.
15 Bert Neugebauer, July 16, 1968.
16 Guyler Magruder.
17 Hal Daugherty, July 19, 1968.
18 George Matkin.
19 Sidney Howard, August 26, 1968; George Matkin, June 28, 1968.
20 *Times,* September 5, 1931.

CHAPTER VIII

Mr. Flory's Boys

1 El Paso *Herald-Post,* June 13, 1932.
2 H. M. Daugherty, July 30, 1968.
3 Mrs. W. W. Wimberly, June 10, 1968.
4 Bert Neugebauer, July 5, 1968.
5 Kenneth Gifford, August 28, 1968.

6 Mrs. W. W. Wimberly.
7 George Matkin, December 27, 1968; Mrs. W. W. Wimberly.
8 Jack Clark, July 30, 1968; Tom Foster, January 15, 1969.
9 Guyler Magruder, July 5, 1968.
10 H. M. Daugherty, July 19, 1968.
11 Kenneth Gifford.
12 *Ibid.*
13 Guyler Magruder.
14 Kenneth Gifford.
15 Mrs. W. W. Wimberly.
16 Myra Bassett Daugherty, August 28, 1968.
17 *Herald-Post,* June 13, 15, 1932; *Times,* June 15, 1932.

CHAPTER IX

Bank Holiday

1 Patterson, *The Great Boom and Panic,* 194.
2 Wecter, *The Age of the Great Depression,* 62.
3 El Paso *Times,* September 19, 1931.
4 *Ibid.,* September 13, 1931.
5 *Ibid.,* September 10, 15, October 3, 1931.
6 *Ibid.,* October 14, 1931.
7 *Ibid.,* December 18, 1932.
8 Leuchtenburg, *Franklin D. Roosevelt and the New Deal,* 38.
9 Schlesinger, *The Coming of the New Deal,* 436-438.
10 Wecter, 54.
11 George Matkin, July 9, 1968.
12 Sidney Howard, August 26, 1968.
13 George Matkin.
14 Mrs. W. W. Wimberly, June 10, 1968.

CHAPTER X

Between the Dark and the Daylight

1 Wecter, *The Age of the Great Depression,* 66-67.
2 Guyler Magruder, July 5, 1968.
3 George Matkin, July 9, 1968.
4 El Paso *Herald-Post,* June 30, 1938.
5 El Paso *Times,* December 31, 1933.
6 *Ibid.,* February 29, August 24, October 7, November 22, December 18, 1932; January 1, 1933.
7 SNB Directors' Minutes, December 29, 1934.
8 Cox, *The State National Bank,* 18.
9 Myra Bassett Daugherty, H. M. Daugherty, August 28, 1968.
10 *Herald-Post,* June 11, 1944.
11 SNB Directors' Minutes.
12 Myra Bassett Daugherty, H. M. Daugherty.
13 *Times,* June 11, 1944.
14 Myra Bassett Daugherty, H. M. Daugherty.
15 *Ibid.*
16 W. W. Scott, June 14, 1968.
17 SNB Directors' Minutes, June 24, 1944.
18 William Hanley, July 26, 1968.
19 *Herald-Post,* August 6, 10, 13, 14, 15, 1945.
20 Cox, 10-13.
21 SNB Directors' Minutes, March 30, 1934, May 27, 1935, May 31, 1941.
22 *Ibid.,* December 14, 1945, October 25, 1948, October 27, 1950.

CHAPTER XI

Back to Prosperity

1 Background information comes from Patricia Reschenthaler, *Postwar Readjustment in El Paso 1945-1950.* El Paso: Texas Western Press, 1968 (Southwestern Studies, No. 21); El Paso County Board of Development, *The Changing Face of El Paso,* El Paso, 1966; El Paso Industrial Development Corporation, *This Is El Paso,* El Paso, 1967.
2 John Richards, *Economic Growth in El Paso, 1950-1962,* 13; El Paso *Herald-Post,* April 11, 1968; *This Is El Paso.*
3 SNB President's report to SNB stockholders, January 28, 1968.
4 SNB, Statement of Condition, June 30, 1970.
5 Hal Stewart, Memorandum to George Matkin, October 31, 1968; Hal Daugherty, July 30, 1968.
6 George Matkin, report to SNB stockholders, January 13, 1959, and later reports.
7 Hal Stewart, Memorandum.
8 William Hanley, July 26, 1968.
9 George Matkin, report to SNB stockholders, January 14, 1958; January 13, 1959.
10 *This Is El Paso.*

11 President's report to SNB stockholders, January 28, 1968.
12 George Matkin, report to SNB stockholders, January, 1962.
13 President's report to SNB stockholders, January 28, 1968.
14 El Paso *Times,* April 23, 1967; Guyler Magruder, July 5, 1968; Jack Clark, July 30, 1968.
15 George Matkin, June 28, 1968.
16 Issues of July 22-28, 1970.
17 George Matkin, reports to stockholders, various dates, supplies information about automation in the bank. Matkin and Daugherty discussed the Chinese and their business on December 30, 1969.
18 Joe Herrera, July 8, 1968.
19 Sidney Howard, August 26, 1968.
20 President's report June 28, 1968; W. W. Scott, August 6, 1970.

CHAPTER XII

Full Service

1 William Purse, July 8, 1968.
2 El Paso *Times,* November 6, 1968.
3 Sidney Howard, August 26, 1968.
4 Mrs. W. W. Wimberly, June 10, 1968.
5 Bert Neugebauer, July 16, 1968.
6 Riley Brown, June 13, 1968.
7 James Alcorn, September 8, 1968.
8 R. E. Austin, June 12, 1968.
9 Raymond Adams, June 25, 1968.
10 Guyler Magruder, July 9, 1968.
11 Doris Ryan, July 23, 1968.
12 Mrs. W. W. Wimberly.
13 Riley Brown.
14 Tom Brennan, July 19, 1968.
15 Sidney Howard; L. R. (Sag) Shea, August 6, 1970. All federally insured banks will be required to install similar equipment by 1971 (*Times,* November 8, 1968).
16 H. M. Daugherty, July 19, 1968.

CHAPTER XIII

The Case of the Missing President

The Lockhart Case was well covered by the El Paso newspapers in the spring, summer and fall of 1969. Items appeared on the following dates:

March 22, 24, 25, 26, 27, 28, 29.

April 2, 3, 4, 5.

May 3.

June 11, 12, 16, 23.

July 3, 4, 7, 8, 10, 11, 25, 26, 30.

October 3.

CHAPTER XIV

New Blood*

1 Lynwood Boyer, July 30, 1970.
2 Plans for the State National-Sharedata Center, were announced October 28, 1970.
3 Martin Kern, July 30, 1870.
4 William Updike, July 24, 1970.
5 *Herald-Post,* December 29, 1970.
6 Hal Daugherty, Jr., July 24, 1970.
7 George Matkin, Hal Daugherty, August 17, 1970.

*In February 1971, Michael R. Moses, a specialist in electronic data processing and accounting systems, became a vice-president in the Marketing Division.

CHAPTER XV

Tallest Bank in Town

Information about the new bank is from the following:

Interviews with George Matkin, H. M. Daugherty, and Walter Scott, especially on December 27, 1968 and with Lynwood Boyer, July 30, 1970.

Fact Sheet, "The New State National Bank Building," May 22, 1969.

Remarks by George Matkin addressed to representatives of El Paso news media, May 23, 1969, at the bank.

News stories, El Paso *Herald-Post,* November 13, December 1, 1965; May 23, 1969; December 23, 1969; January 15, 1970; April 6, 1970; El Paso *Times,* May 22, 24, 1969; December 23, 1969. February 1, September 20, November 18, 1970.

INDEX